W9-ACW-136

The Effective Teacher's Guide to Autism and Communication Difficulties

In this welcome second edition of *The Effective Teacher's Guide to Autism and Communication Difficulties*, best-selling author Michael Farrell addresses how teachers and others can develop provision for students with autism and students that have difficulties with speech, grammar, meaning, use of language and comprehension. Updated and expanded, this book allows the teacher to be self-critical in developing classroom approaches and offers up-to-date research combined with professional experience on how to best achieve good practice in the classroom. This accessible book offers down-to-earth information on:

- terms and definitions;
- legal considerations;
- classroom strategies;
- useful resources;
- pedagogical issues.

This new edition will be a useful source of ideas and guidance for teachers and others working with children with autism or other communication disorders. It will also be useful for all new teachers, for those continuing professional development, school managers and administrators.

Michael Farrell is a widely published private special education consultant. He works with children, families, schools, local authorities, voluntary organisations, universities and government ministries. He has published books extensively with Routledge with recent titles including *The Special Education Handbook* (4th edition) and *Debating Special Education*.

The Effective Teacher's Guides Series, all by Michael Farrell

The Effective Teacher's Guide to Behavioural and Emotional Disorders: Disruptive behaviour disorders, anxiety disorders and depressive disorders, and attention deficit hyperactivity disorder, 2nd edition
PB: 978-0-415-56568-4 (Published 2010)

The Effective Teacher's Guide to Sensory and Physical Impairments: Sensory, orthopaedic, motor and health impairments, and traumatic brain injury, 2nd edition
PB: 978-0-415-56565-3 (Published 2010)

The Effective Teacher's Guide to Autism and Communication Difficulties, 2nd edition
PB: 978-0-415-69383-7 (Published 2012)

The Effective Teacher's Guide to Dyslexia and other Specific Learning Difficulties (Learning Disabilities), 2nd edition
PB: 978-0-415-69385-1 (Published 2012)

The Effective Teacher's Guide to Moderate, Severe and Profound Learning Difficulties (Cognitive Impairments), 2nd edition
PB: 978-0-415-69387-5 (Published 2012)

The Effective Teacher's Guide to Autism and Communication Difficulties

Practical strategies

Second edition

Michael Farrell

 Routledge
Taylor & Francis Group

LONDON AND NEW YORK

GUELPH HUMBER LIBRARY
205 Humber College Blvd
Toronto, ON M9W 5L7

First published 2006 by Routledge
This second edition published 2012
by Routledge
2 Park Square, Milton Park, Abingdon, Oxon OX14 4RN

Simultaneously published in the USA and Canada
by Routledge
711 Third Avenue, New York, NY 10017

Routledge is an imprint of the Taylor & Francis Group, an informa business

British Library Cataloguing in Publication Data
A catalogue record for this book is available from the British Library

Library of Congress Cataloging in Publication Data
Farrell, Michael, 1948–
The effective teacher's guide to autism and communication difficulties:
practical strategies / Michael Farrell. – 2nd ed.
p. cm. – (The Effective Teacher's Guides)
Includes bibliographical references and index.
1. Autistic children – Education. 2. Autistic children – Language. 3.
Autism in children. 4. Communicative disorders in children. I. Title.
LC4717.F37 2012
371.94 – dc23
2011024838

ISBN: 978-0-415-69382-0 (hbk)
ISBN: 978-0-415-69383-7 (pbk)
ISBN: 978-0-203-15288-1 (ebk)

Typeset in Bembo
by Taylor & Francis Books

Contents

Preface to second edition

I am of course extremely pleased to be writing the preface to the second edition of this book, *The Effective Teacher's Guide to Autism and Communication Difficulties: Practical Strategies.* The previous edition, published in 2006, attracted favourable comment and I have listened to the views of readers about how the edition might be improved.

I hope it continues to be useful and I again welcome comments from readers to ensure any future editions are as informative and helpful as possible.

Michael Farrell
Herefordshire
dr.m.j.farrell@btopenworld.com

The author

Michael Farrell was educated in the United Kingdom. After training as a teacher at Bishop Grosseteste College, Lincoln, and obtaining an honours degree from Nottingham University, he was awarded a master's degree in Education and Psychology from the Institute of Education, London University. Subsequently, he gained a Master of Philosophy degree at the Institute of Psychiatry, Maudsley Hospital, London, and a Doctor of Philosophy degree under the auspices of the Medical Research Council Cognitive Development Unit and London University.

Professionally, Michael Farrell has worked as a head teacher, a lecturer at London University and as a local authority inspector. He managed a national psychometric project for City University, London and directed a national teacher education project for the United Kingdom Government Department of Education. His present role as a private special education consultant includes work with children and families, schools, local authorities, voluntary organisations, universities and government departments in Britain and elsewhere.

His many books, translated into European and Asian languages, include:

- *Foundations of Special Education: An Introduction* (Wiley, 2009);
- *The Special Education Handbook* (4th edition) (David Fulton, 2009);
- *Debating Special Education* (Routledge, 2010).

Chapter 1

Introduction

This chapter sets the book in the context of the series of which it forms a part. It explains the features of the new edition. I outline the types of disorders with which the book is concerned. The chapter then provides preliminary information that will be helpful to reading later chapters. I then describe the content of subsequent chapters. I suggest potential readers likely to find the book useful.

The Effective Teachers' Guides

'The Effective Teachers' Guides' published by Routledge concern different types of disabilities and disorders. These include cognitive impairment ('learning difficulties' in the United Kingdom and 'mental retardation' in the United States of America), autism, emotional and behavioural disorders, reading disorder/dyslexia and others. Each book in the series describes practical strategies that enable the educational progress and personal and social development of pupils with particular disabilities and disorders.

The titles are:

The Effective Teacher's Guide to Behavioural and Emotional Disorders: Disruptive behaviour disorders, anxiety disorders and depressive disorders, and attention deficit hyperactivity disorder (2nd edition);

The Effective Teacher's Guide to Sensory and Physical Impairments: Sensory, orthopaedic, motor and health impairments, and traumatic brain injury (2nd edition);

The Effective Teacher's Guide to Autism and Communication Difficulties (2nd edition);

The Effective Teacher's Guide to Moderate, Severe and Profound Learning Difficulties (Cognitive Impairment) (2nd edition);

The Effective Teacher's Guide to Dyslexia and other Learning Difficulties (Learning Disabilities) (2nd edition).

The new edition

The Effective Teacher's Guide to Autism and Communication Difficulties is the second edition of a book previously published in 2006. The first edition was generously reviewed and well received by readers. This new edition seeks to make the content more widely accessible to readers in different countries.

The 2006 edition was set within the context of legislation and procedures in the United Kingdom. The new edition focuses more on strategies that work without undue reference to a particular national context.

Autism and communication disorders

This chapter outlines types of difficulties and disorders with which the book is concerned. These are derived from classifications used in the United Kingdom and the United States of America. The chapter then outlines the contents of the subsequent chapters and describes the proposed readers.

In the United States of America, pupils considered to need special education covered by federal law both have a defined disability, and are considered to need special education because the disability has an adverse educational impact. Categories of disability under federal law as amended in 1997 (20 United States Code 1402, 1997) are reflected in 'designated disability codes' and include the following:

- speech and language impaired;
- autism.

In England, a similar classification (Department for Education and Skills, 2005, *passim*) includes:

- speech, language and communication needs;
- autistic spectrum disorder.

In the present book, chapters look at disorders of speech, grammar, comprehension, semantics (meaning), pragmatics (use) and at autism. (For an overview of child language disorders, see Schwartz, 2007.) I hope looking at communication disorders and autism in this way allows teachers to improve a child's communication through familiar curriculum opportunities as well as specific programmes. This educational typology reflects the training and expertise of teachers and others.

The teacher and the speech pathologist

The perspectives of a speech and language pathologist (the term used predominantly in the United States of America, Australia and Canada) or speech therapist (the expression often employed in the United Kingdom) is important. It is informed by, among other factors, their particular training and expertise. Among the ways in which this may be reflected is in the frameworks for understanding that are used regarding speech and language development, pathology and remediation. A speech pathologist may take a psycholinguistic perspective of communication. Such frameworks are in turn reflected in terminology which may often refer to clinical conditions such as dysarthria, verbal dyspraxia, dysphonia, dysphasia and so on. These terms are explained later.

Where educational and speech pathology perspectives do not overlap, the teacher and speech pathologist, school psychologist and others will need to work closely together. The purpose is to ensure that their aims coincide and that the educational and speech pathology terminology and perspectives are meshed together with regard to proposed interventions.

Form and content

Townsend (1997), writing in the context of aesthetics, suggests that any-thing produced by humans to have a meaning implies 'some distinction between form and content' (ibid. p. 57). Sentences have a form and also convey something to a listener or reader. The form of a sentence includes its grammar and the 'system of meanings that are attached to each word and to combinations of words in a language' (ibid.). An example of the form of a sentence is the noun phrase consisting of a simple noun, or a noun and an adjective, or a pronoun. The form can be described in a way that 'does not require us to say what the sentence means' (ibid.).

Grammar concerns form. Other aspects concern meaning, including the area of study known as semantics. Form and content, while convenient ways of helping us analyse language, always occur together. There can be no form without content and no content without form. Neither form nor content can exist alone. Although for convenience, I separately consider speech, grammar, comprehension, semantics (meaning) and pragmatics (use), they are intimately related.

Delay and disorder

A distinction may be made between language delay and language dis-order. With language delay, language is similar to that expected of a younger child. Language disorder is different to what is expected both qualitatively and quantitatively. But the distinction is not clear-cut.

A child may use sounds, words and structures associated with a younger child. But it is not always possible without the power of foresight to determine whether development is delayed or atypical. Later the child may develop language typical of his age when it would be possible looking back to recognise that earlier language patterns were delayed. On the other hand the child may not develop in this way and problems may continue in which case it would be justifiable looking back to say that earlier language might have been disordered. In other words, the confirmation of delay or disorder may be a retrospective assessment.

Some language difficulties appear to be related to other developmental difficulties, for example learning difficulties or hearing impairment. Other language difficulties do not appear to be related to other developmental difficulties. Where poor language development is discrepant with other more age typical levels of development, then the term 'specific language impairment/difficulties' may be used (Adams *et al.*, 1997).

Within child and contextual explanations

There is discussion about terms which might suggest that the difficulty is predominantly within child or mainly environmental/contextual. The term 'impairment' is sometimes taken to imply a within child explanation. Consequently, the expression language 'needs' may be preferred.

However, the word 'needs' raises difficulties too. While it might be taken to place greater emphasis on environmental factors, it does not make it clear how the supposed 'needs' arise nor who decides what the needs are. If the needs arise from predominantly within child factors, then the term is merely a euphemism for impairment. Of course, 'need' implies that provision should be made but this is superfluous given this is the purpose of special education.

A framework for communication disorders

A framework for communication disorders is the *Diagnostic and Statistical Manual of Mental Disorders Fourth Edition Text Revision* (*DSM-IV-TR*) (American Psychiatric Association, 2000). The delineation of communication disorders (ibid., pp. 58–69) comprises:

- expressive language disorder;
- mixed expressive-receptive language disorder;
- phonological disorder;

- stuttering;
- communication disorder not otherwise specified.

(In the United Kingdom the term 'stammer' is often used instead of 'stutter'.)

Expressive language disorder is an impairment in expressive language development. An indicator is that standardised assessment scores for expressive language are substantially below standardised scores for non-verbal intellectual capacity and for receptive language. Functional assessments are also made. Features of expressive language disorder may include a limited amount of speech and range of vocabulary; limited types of grammatical structures; and difficulty acquiring new words. The child with expressive language disorder may have problems with 'word finding'. This means he can recognise a word and understand it, but has difficulty producing a needed word in conversation or when shown a picture. The difficulty appears to be in accessing/retrieving the words (Dockrell et al., 1998). The most common associated feature of expressive language disorder is phonological disorder.

Mixed expressive-receptive language disorder is an impairment of both expressive and receptive language development. It is indicated by scores for these areas of development on standardised tests being substantially below those for intellectual capacity. Features are similar to those for expressive language disorder with the addition of a comprehension deficit. As with expressive language disorder, function assessments may be made. A child's receptive problems may be missed in the classroom because the child may copy others and appear to manage adequately.

Phonological disorder involves a child failing to develop speech sounds appropriate for his age and dialect. It may involve errors in, 'sound production, use, representation, or organisation ... ' (American Psychiatric Association, 2000, p. 65). Phonological disorder includes difficulties with phonological production and cognitively based forms of phonological problems. These involve a 'deficit in linguistic categorisation of speech sounds' (ibid. p. 65). The disorder may involve errors in the selection and ordering of sounds within syllables and words. It is more common in boys than girls. These difficulties impede academic or occupational achievement or social communication. Types of phonological disorder include developmental verbal dyspraxia and dysarthria. In some frameworks, the difficulties just outlined are considered motor/speech articulation problems rather than phonological disorders.

Stuttering involves a disturbance of 'normal fluency and time patterning of speech'. It is inappropriate for the individual's age and typified by repetitions or prolongations of sounds or syllables. Stuttering interferes with academic or occupational achievement or social communication. A child or young person who stutters may have particular difficulties communicating with peers. Prevalence is about 1 per cent in children and around 0.8 per cent in adolescents (American Psychiatric Association, 2000, p. 67) and the male:female ratio is around 3 to 1. In about 98 per cent of instances stuttering begins before the age of 10 years. There is strong evidence of a genetic factor (ibid., p. 68) as well as evidence that many factors contribute. (See www.nsastutter.org/index.php for the National Stuttering Association [United States of America] and www.stammering. org for the British Stammering Association.) A therapy manual by Stewart and Turnbull (2007) offers practical approaches for dysfluency.

Within the *DSM-IV-TR* (American Psychiatric Association, 2000) framework, communication disorder 'not otherwise specified' includes voice disorder such as an abnormality of vocal pitch or loudness.

Developmental verbal dyspraxia and dysarthria

Developmental verbal dyspraxia is also called 'apraxia of speech'. While it involves no obvious muscular abnormality, it is a difficulty 'in initiating, in directing and in controlling the speed and duration of movements of articulation' (Milloy and MorganBarry, 1990, p. 121). It affects the child's ability to coordinate the speech organs in order to produce sounds accurately.

The child may avoid speaking because of difficulties with speech, particularly at speed. He will require support, encouragement and practice before being able to 'incorporate new sounds into syllables at normal speed' (Kirby and Drew, 2003, p. 135). Speech may be 'slow or halting, and sometimes it appears to be a struggle to talk' (ibid. pp. 134–5). Often there are problems with vowels. These may be the main factor hindering progress for speech intelligibility and literacy, especially spelling. There may be associated difficulties in language and literacy skills (Stackhouse and Wells, 1997). There is debate about the extent to which developmental verbal dyspraxia may relate to immature neural development.

Dysarthria is an 'impairment of movement and coordination of the muscles required for speech, due to abnormal muscle tone' (Milloy and MorganBarry, 1990, p. 109). It may be a feature of multiple sclerosis and cerebral palsy. Physical factors can affect speech at different levels.

Neurological damage brought about by head injury or by brain damage before, during or soon after birth can sometimes lead to physical disabilities with associated speech difficulties. Neurological disease such as meningitis or brain tumour can be associated with speech difficulties, which may be progressive. Poor motor skills and poor coordination may lead to slurred articulation. Neurologically based speech difficulties may be so severe that non-speech based communication has to be used.

Other terms

Further terminology includes:

- aphasia: an absence of previously acquired language skills brought about by a brain disorder affecting the ability to speak and write and/or comprehend and read. The expression is sometimes used interchangeably with dysphasia (Tesak and Code, 2007);
- dysphasia: a disturbance of language skills. Developmental dysphasia refers to a language disturbance apparently lacking a clear environmental cause. Acquired dysphasia refers to the loss of previously competent language skills through a trauma such as a road traffic accident;
- Anomia: word finding difficulties (in the United Kingdom, 'anomia' tends to be used with reference to adults and 'word finding difficulties' is used with reference to children) (Laine and Martin, 2006);
- dysphonia: defects of the sound system caused by disease of or damage to the larynx (voice box).

The broader term 'specific language impairment' describes children with a range of language profiles involving combinations of deficits in phonology, syntax, morphology, semantics and pragmatics. There are marked language difficulties but the cause is not evident and the child has normal cognitive abilities (Leonard, 1998, *passim*). This excludes children with autism (which is classified as a pervasive disorder not a specific one), general cognitive deficits and physical or neurological damage (e.g. head injury, cleft palate, cerebral palsy).

Having considered the framework for communication disorders in the *DSM-IV-TR* and briefly described developmental verbal dyspraxia and dysarthria and other terms, we are now in a position to consider different aspects of speech difficulties. These are the subject of the next chapter.

Subsequent chapters

Subsequent chapters concern the following topics:

Chapter 2 Communication disorders: speech;
Chapter 3 Communication disorders: grammar;

Each chapter defines and discusses the condition being considered. I then consider provision with regard to: the curriculum and assessment, pedagogy, resources, organization and therapy. This is followed by a section giving suggestions for further reading. The book includes a bibliography and a combined subject and author index.

Proposed readers

I hope readers will include the following:

- teachers and other professionals in mainstream schools, special schools and other settings;
- student teachers and teachers in the early years after qualification;
- parents;
- school managers and administrators;
- anyone interested in provision for children and young people with communication difficulties or autism.

Further reading

Farrell, M. (2009b) (4th edition) *The Special Education Handbook* London, David Fulton.

The book includes entries specific to communication disorders and autism.

Kauffman, J. M. and Hallahan, D. P. (2005) *Special Education: What It Is and Why We Need It* Boston, MA, Pearson/Allyn and Bacon.

This introductory but well-argued book sets out the case for special education and explains some of its main features.

Reynolds, C. R. and Fletcher-Janzen, E. (Eds) (2004) (2nd edition) *Concise Encyclopaedia of Special Education: A Reference for the Education of Handicapped and Other Exceptional Children and Adults* Hoboken, NY, John Wiley and Sons.

This reference work includes reviews of assessment instruments, biographies, teaching approaches and overviews of disabilities and disorders.

Chapter 2

Communication disorders
Speech

INTRODUCTION

This chapter considers speech difficulties and their identification and assessment. Next I examine aspects of speech difficulties: phonetic, prosodic and phonological. Then the chapter looks at provision for phonological disorders in terms of curriculum and assessment, pedagogy, resources, therapy and organisation.

Speech difficulties

Speech and language are not synonymous. Speech is only one form of language, the spoken form, others being writing or signs. Thompson (2003, p. 10) defines speech as 'the mechanical aspect of communication ... the ability to produce the sounds, words and phrases'.

Speech difficulties can be considered to occur when communication is impaired by the child's capacity for speech. Among reasons why speech may be unintelligible are:

- physical difficulties with articulation; and/or
- difficulties making sound contrasts that convey meaning; and/or
- problems in controlling pitch.

These three difficulties are aspects respectively of:

- phonetics;
- phonology;
- prosody.

Each of these aspects is considered later.

The identification and assessment of speech difficulties

Parent, teacher and speech pathologist

Turning to identification and assessment, parents may be the first to notice their child's speech problems. The teacher may also have concerns. It is important to remember that speech and language are intertwined so that slow progress with language can be associated with delayed speech. Consider a young child who appears to have speech problems and says very little. With such a child, it may be a useful strategy to focus on developing vocabulary and syntax.

You may suspect difficulties when considering the pupil's attainments and progress in relation to usual developmental milestones. You may notice delays with regard to age-typical curriculum achievements in speaking and listening. Routine screening procedures and other assessments such as checklists used by the school may suggest slow progress.

Such indications will be informed by the teacher's experience and knowledge of typical child development. They may lead you to consult a senior colleague. You might both agree to keep the child's progress under review, discussing the concerns with parents and gaining their perspective. The teacher may arrange to carry out further assessments including standardised ones.

You may seek advice from the speech pathologist/therapist who may observe the child and carry out specialist assessments. The speech pathologist may look at sound production in single words and in continuous speech. This should help establish whether the child can make every individual sound in their spoken language, then in single words and in continuous speech.

Assessing speech sounds in different language contexts

Issues arise in connection with assessments of speech sounds in different language contexts:

- in isolation;
- in a syllable;
- in a word;
- in connected, perhaps conversational speech.

Assessments of individual speech sounds are sometimes carried out to measure the speed and accuracy of the child's articulation. This can indicate whether the child has difficulties coordinating speech muscles.

Some children may be able to make an individual speech sound (e.g. 'b') but be unable to make the sound in a word ('big', 'rib' and 'robber'). When assessing speech sounds in a syllable, single syllable words may be used in which the sound to be assessed is the initial or final sound and is minimally influenced by the other sounds of the syllable. Assessing a speech sound in a word, perhaps by asking the child to name a picture, may be more natural than assessing the sound in isolation. However, other speech sounds in the word may influence the target one. The pathologist and the teacher therefore carefully choose the words and the position of the focus speech sound within it. For example the sound of the 's' in the words 'saw' and 'straw' are influenced by the sound that follows the initial 's'.

If speech sounds are assessed as they occur in regular speech, this is more natural, but again the target sound may be influenced by the other sounds in the words used. Consequently, conversational speech should be analysed carefully perhaps by recoding it for later analysis. If this is done in different contexts such as school and home it gives the opportunity for the teacher, the parent and the speech pathologist to pool information and coordinate approaches. Yet, it is pertinent to remember that the speech pathologist is the professional who is particularly trained to carry out a detailed analysis of the sound system.

Distinguishing possible speech difficulties from other issues

Speech difficulties need to be distinguished from problems with grammar. Take for example a speech difficulty involving the sound 's'. This may make it hard for the child to indicate grammatical features such as plural endings (coat/coats) even if he knows them. But other children may similarly tend not to indicate such endings even though they are able to make the necessary sound 's'. They may not understand the grammatical convention. Consider a situation in which interventions are made for phonological disorders, and speech improves because of successful interventions. This may reveal that the pupil has other difficulties, for example to do with grammar, which have previously been masked by the speech difficulties.

Children with speech disorders finding it difficult to communicate may become very frustrated. They may be reluctant to communicate or refuse to try. If required to communicate, they become intensely anxious. The child may feel low self-esteem and may feel rejected by peers. Indeed he may be rejected or bullied by some. (See the Cleft Lip and Palate Association at www.clapa.com and the American Cleft Palate Foundation at www.cleftline.org.) In this context, the child may develop emotional and behavioural problems. Recognising such pres sures, the teacher, parents, speech pathologist and others will liaise closely to ensure the pupil is supported emotionally and socially.

You need to be careful not to assume a pupil's speech difficulties indicate a general difficulty with learning. This can risk expecting too little progress of the child. If other pupils are allowed to make a similar assumption, their interactions with the pupil may similarly dampen expectations. This can hinder progress and willingness to learn. Also, direct efforts to help the pupil communicate intelligibly are more likely to improve skills and self-esteem.

Children who speak English as an additional language and who experience speech difficulties may manifest difficulties in either their first language or English or both. Therefore it is necessary to assess in both languages before suitable strategies can be determined. Speech pathologists may be bilingual or work with co-workers who are bilingual or interpreters.

Aspects of speech difficulties: phonetic, prosodic and phonological

It was stated earlier that three aspects of speech difficulties may be identified relating to phonetics, prosody and phonology.

- Phonetics is the study of articulation.
- Prosody is an aspect of phonetics concerning such speech features as volume and changes in pitch.
- Phonology concerns differences in speech sounds that carry meaning.

These are interrelated aspects of speech although the causes of speech difficulties and intervention sometimes relate to one aspect more specifically than another.

Phonetics and phonetic difficulties

Phonetics is the study of articulation, a form of motor skill learning. It leads to the automatic moving of speech articulators in the mouth in 'rapid, precise and co-ordinated sequences' (Martin and Miller, 2003, p. 27). Phonetic aspects of speech include the speech sounds that can be segmented into the components of their articulation and into consonants and vowels.

Articulation problems arise when motor skills are insufficient to produce the sounds for speech. This may be caused by physical disability if this affects learning motor skills necessary for speech. One physical cause is cleft lip and cleft palate, which can be brought about by drugs or viruses (e.g. rubella) in early pregnancy. These conditions can be treated surgically. Children with cleft lip/palate may also be at risk of having hearing problems and delayed language development. Muscular dystrophy can lead to deterioration in speech skill. Cerebral palsy may be associated with neurological effects on oral movements affecting articulation.

Hearing impairment may cause articulatory difficulties, and children with intermittent hearing loss/ glue ear can have speech problems. Dysphonia is a difficulty with voicing in which there is no voice at all or it is croaky. Among its causes are congenital malformation of the vocal chord and abnormalities in the structure of the larynx. Other causes are paralysis of the vocal chords from accident, or genetic factors related to certain syndromes. More obviously, voice problems can be caused by the abuse or overuse of the voice, for example by excessive shouting (Hunt and Slater, 2003, *passim*).

Prosody and prosodic difficulties

Prosody is an aspect of phonetics concerning features of speech. These include volume, patterns of intonation and changes in pitch. They can indicate, for example, questions, feeling and surprise. Prosody also involves the rhythm and fluency of speech, which help convey meaning, helping the listener understand.

A phoneme is the smallest phonetic unit that can carry meaning. It distinguishes one word from another. In the words 'cat' and 'cap', the sounds for 't' and 'p' are phonemes. In literacy phoneme-grapheme awareness is clearly important. Onset and rime are units smaller than a syllable but larger than a phoneme.

- The 'onset' corresponds to the opening part of the syllable.
- The 'rime' contains the peak (or vowel nucleus) and the coda (the phonemes that come after it) (Howell and Dean, 1994, p. 94).

When learning a new word, speakers attend especially to the onset and to the beat of the syllables. Therefore, when teaching children new vocabulary, it helps to draw particular attention to these two features. Prosodic aspects of speech can affect the meaning of a complete utterance, as when the intonation is raised at the end of an utterance to indicate a question. Such instances have an effect at the phonological level of speech.

Prosodic difficulties concern such speech features as volume, patterns of intonation and changes in pitch, rhythm and fluency. A child with prosodic difficulties may also have problems with the use of language (pragmatics).

Stuttering or stammering is a difficulty with fluency that can make it more difficult for a listener to fully understand what is being said. Dysfluency disrupts the prosodic features of communication. A child who stammers is normally referred to a speech pathologist at an early age. It is less usual for stammering to occur in adolescence. Where it does so, social and emotional factors may be implicated. The teacher would be likely to seek advice from a senior colleague; and a speech pathologist may be consulted.

Phonology and phonological difficulties

Essentially, phonology concerns the differences in speech sounds that carry meaning. Definitions can be very broad. Watson (1991) states phonology refers to 'all the sound related aspects of language, knowledge and behaviour' (ibid. p. 26). Focusing on the systems concerning speech sounds Martin (2000) asserts phonology comprises 'the system with rules to organise speech sounds into sequences to make words' (ibid. p. 14).

Phonological knowledge enables the speaker to understand that, when a speech sound is changed in a word, meaning changes. Speakers come to learn distinctions such as 'dog'/'log' or 'pin'/'pig'. The speaker hears his own speech and modifies it as necessary to make the required word. The phonological system appears to lay down a sort of cognitive phonological representation of the speech-sound sequence. This is part of what enables the process to be automatic. Speakers can draw on this phonological representation when they are developing awareness of the different sounds in a word. (In reading in English, the 44 speech sounds are linked to written marks or graphemes so that the child develops a phoneme-grapheme correspondence.) Typically, by 4 years old about 90 per cent of a child's speech is intelligible to a stranger (Law et al., 2000, p. 18).

With phonological problems, there is a difficulty in relating speech sounds to changes in meaning. There may be no obvious cause of the child's unintelligibility and a restricted speech sound system. Yet the child's development of the use of speech sounds to convey meaning has become idiosyncratic. Those who know the child well may still be able to understand much of what the child wants to convey but others will not.

Phonological difficulties and dyspraxia are distinguished. Those familiar with a child with phonological problems understand their speech mainly because there is consistency in the sound patterns the child uses. However, with dyspraxia, there is a lack of consistency making it difficult to understand the child. The child's speech profile may be specific or delayed or a mixture of the two. Specific and delayed profiles are managed differently (see also, Lancaster and Pope, 1997, passim).

Provision for phonological disorders

Curriculum and assessment

The curriculum is likely to help pupils with phonological disorders if it emphasises speaking and listening, as an activity in English lessons and as an important aspect of all other lessons. Structured sessions may be organised focusing on improving phonological skills and knowledge. More broadly, planning will ensure that in all aspects of the curriculum, phonological development is taken into account and supported. More time may be spent on developing phonology across the curriculum. Special programmes may be included in provision such as Metaphon described later.

Phonological development may be assessed in small steps to provide the opportunity to recognise progress.

Pedagogy

Raising phonological awareness

Raising phonological awareness lends itself to whole class and small group teaching and can be interesting for all pupils including those with speech disorders. It is also an important part of the overall curriculum and literacy development. Where you introduce new vocabulary, you will try to encourage a keen interest in the word or phrase. You will need to explicitly teach and check the pupils' understanding of various aspects of the vocabulary.

These include:

- phonological – how do the sounds of the word break up and blend back together? Do the pupils know any similar sounding words? What are the syllables of the word? (Younger pupils may enjoy clapping them out.)
- grammatical – how is the word used in sentences?
- semantic – what does the word mean? Does it have interesting origins?

This can be routinely and briefly accomplished, for example, if key words are introduced at the beginning of a lesson. In schools, teachers other than English specialists can use the approach to reinforce new vocabulary. These strategies are also important for children with word finding difficulties.

Encouraging phonological change

Several programmes or resources aim to encourage phonological change. The Children's Phonology Sourcebook (Flynn and Lancaster, 1997) is intended for speech pathologists but provides ideas and resources that can be copied for parents and teachers. Coverage includes auditory input, first words, speech perception and phonological representations. It emphasises the auditory processing of speech. (See www.speechmark.net.)

Metaphon uses activities designed to bring about phonological change (Howell and Dean, 1994, p. vii). The Metaphon Resource Pack (Dean *et al.*, 1990), used mainly by speech pathologists with children aged 3½ to 7 years, provides phonological assessment. Therapeutic activities include practising and playing with language, for example, rhyming activities and spontaneous use of 'repairs' to communication.

Error analysis and articulation exercises

Error analysis assumes a child acquiring speech progressively develops sounds that become increasingly like those made by adults. Speech difficulty, it is believed, involves the child having selected the wrong sound, hence the term 'error' analysis. The child is therefore taught the 'correct' sound. A child may pronounce words like 'yes' and 'mess' as 'yeth' and 'meth' and yet have no apparent phonological difficulty. The teacher or speech pathologist helps the child recognise the sound the child is making and the distinction between it and the target sound. Articulation exercises are used to develop and encourage the correct sound. There may of course also be an articulation problem.

On the negative side, the approach seems to suggest speech sounds are rather isolated from the meaning of language. There is an implication speech sounds develop individually rather than within a complex context of the child trying to convey meaning, and cultural and media influences. An alternative view is that the motivation for the child to be increasingly precise in making speech sounds is the desire to be understood. Encouraging that motivation is therefore important if the child is to develop increasingly precise speech sounds.

Where error analysis is used, the interventions may include exercises for breathing, swallowing and articulation. Activities may be designed to improve the child's awareness of speech mechanisms and gaining control over the lips, tongue, palate and breathing. Such activities are used when the problem is identified as an articulation/motor speech problem. They might include licking round the lips and modelling movements for the child to copy. The intention is to raise awareness and improve underlying muscular control. Specific sounds may be taught using a progressive approach. This ranges from teaching and using the sound:

* in isolation;
* in nonsense syllables;
* in initial and final positions in simple consonant-vowel-consonant words;
* in medial position;
* in consonant blends.

Cued articulation is also used as a teaching support for children with speech problems.

Alternative and augmentative communication

Where alternative and augmentative communication is used for children with speech problems the problems tend to be very severe. (For an overview see Cockerill and Carrollfew, 2007.) Alternative and augmentative communication may be non-aided or aided.

'Non-aided' communication involves the child making a movement or vocalisation that does not necessitate a physical aid or other device (Vanderheiden and Lloyd, 1986). Examples are oral language, manual sign languages or individualised communication (e.g. one blink for 'yes' and two for 'no'). A sign language is a system of communication using bodily signs: hand and finger movements, facial expressions and bodily movements.

Among signing methods is the Paget-Gorman sign system, designed to closely parallel the grammar of spoken English. It is intended to complement speech and enhance the ability to write grammatically correctly. Signing may be used as means of communication other than speech or accompany developing speech.

'Aided' communication involves using a device or item other than one's own body such as communication boards, eye gaze boards and electronic systems. Examples are discussed in the section below on resources.

Resources

This section gives a few examples of resources used to help communication, particularly where problems are severe.

Symbols

Computer technology, using symbols, allows a large number of symbols to be used flexibly. There are symbol e-mail programmes, and websites that use symbols. Among commercially available symbols sets are Rebus symbols and Blissymbols. The Picture Exchange Communication System may also be used. Care is needed to ensure that the pupil makes the link between the real and intended object, activity or person and the symbol.

Communication notebook

A communication notebook can include photographs, symbols and words. It enables a pupil to find a symbol and show the particular page to someone who may not know the symbol so they can see the intended word.

Communication grid

A communication grid is a device in which several symbols can be set out in a specified order to enable a pupil to participate in group sessions. For example, it can support retelling a story. A sequence of symbols can be used to indicate a sequence of activities, including a school timetable for a pupil.

Talking mats

Talking mats were developed by the research team at the Alternative and Augmentative Communication Research Unit at the University of Stirling, Scotland. They are used to supplement communication with children and adults. A textured mat is used to which symbols can be attached covering issues, emotions and influences. The use of these symbols in sorted sets allows communication including choices and preferences (www.speechmag.com/archives).

Communication aids for pupils with motor difficulties

For children with motor difficulties, an important consideration is how the child will indicate a selection. This may be done by pointing, using a head stick, eye pointing or light pointing. Other important considerations are the vocabulary content available and the output method (Bigge et al., 2001, pp. 242–50).

Dedicated communication devices

Dedicated communication devices are electronic systems that speak programmed messages when the user activates locations marked by symbols. Computer based communication systems may consist of a computer with input options, communication software and a speech synthesizer. The pupil may have a voice production device having a computer based bank of words and sentences that can be produced by pressing the keyboard keys.

Therapy

Speech and language therapy

The role and contribution of the speech pathologist is important for children with phonological difficulties, whether the pathologist works directly with the child or takes a more advisory or supervisory role. Individual task based programmes may be developed jointly with the teacher and speech pathologist.

Or the speech pathologist might work with a teaching assistant who continues the planned work when the pathologist is not present. The programmes may imply a psycholinguistic perspective focusing on cognitive and linguistic processing (Stackhouse and Wells, 1997).

A psycholinguistic framework can help in understanding and interpreting speech (and literacy) difficulties (Stackhouse and Wells, 1997; Stackhouse and Wells, 2001; Pascoe *et al.*, 2006). Other approaches may be used with a psycholinguistic perspective including phonological approaches and articulatory ones. For children with persisting speech difficulties, such an eclectic approach may be effective (Pascoe *et al.*, 2006, pp. 15–17).

A psycholinguistic perspective

The assessment of a child's difficulties is identified at different levels. Consider a pupil who may have a difficulty receiving and recognising speech input because of a problem with auditory discrimination. Let us assume an audiological assessment indicates hearing loss is not contributing to the speech difficulties. It may be judged that if auditory discrimination were improved, the pupil would be unlikely to have further difficulties with: the processes of storing information; accessing and retrieving knowledge of phonological representations; and transforming this knowledge into speech. The focus for intervention would therefore be on improving auditory discrimination.

But, because the levels are interrelated, work would continue at other levels too. The task based programme might include activities in which the pupil listens to (perhaps recorded) sounds. At first, these would be obviously different but would gradually become more similar. This encourages careful attention to sounds and helps improve auditory discrimination.

Medical/surgical interventions

The school needs to be aware of any previous, ongoing or proposed medical interventions as these can have an impact on the pupil's progress. Surgery may be used for example to treat cleft palate and cleft lip and for chronic middle ear infections. Many operations will be completed before the child starts school. However, continuing hospital appointments and check ups and the associated absences from school make it important that the child's learning is well supported. Medication such as antibiotics may be prescribed for persistent ear infections.

Organisation

If speech problems are very severe or where there are multiple communication problems, signing may be used. Where signing is used, the classroom may be organised so all pupils are able to see the communications and hear the accompanying words. Where a child's speech intelligibility is developing, in group and class settings it will be important that the acoustics are good so everyone can hear what the child is saying. It is also helpful to provide the correct model of the word rather than correcting a child. For example, a child may say 'gog' for 'dog'. The teacher might say, 'You've got a new dog' rather than, 'No, it's not "gog", its "dog"'.

Environmental arrangement strategies involve rearranging the environment to increase the likelihood the pupil will communicate. A desired object may be placed out of reach, the teacher may not give enough objects or pieces to complete a task or the pupil may be offered a choice of items or activities (Kaiser, 2000).

THINKING POINTS

Readers may wish to consider:

- how best to ensure whole school structures that enable the teacher, speech pathologist/therapist and others to work together and liaise;
- how to prioritise the focus for liaison, for example in the development of individual education plans, joint assessment, planning and intervention.

KEY TEXTS

Cockerill, H. and Carrollfew, L. (2007) *Communicating without Speech: Practical Augmentative and Alternative Communication for Children* New York, Blackwell Publishing.

Intended mainly for health professionals such as speech and language pathologists, this book is also relevant for teachers. It concerns children who do not develop adequate speech because of complex neurological conditions or learning disabilities and may require alternative and augmentative communication systems.

Pascoe, M., Stackhouse, J. and Wells, B. (2006) *Children's Speech and Literacy Difficulties* Book 3: *Persisting Speech Difficulties in Children* London, Wiley.

The previous two books in the series concerned respectively an introduction to a psycholinguistic framework, and a focus on identification and assessment.

Chapter 3

Communication disorders
Grammar

INTRODUCTION

This chapter considers grammar and how it develops in children of different ages. I look at causal factors. The chapter examines difficulties with syntax and morphology and considers the assessment of grammar. I look at provision in terms of: curriculum and assessment, pedagogy (sentence recasting, elicited imitation, modelling and clear teacher communication), resources, therapy and organisation.

Grammar and its development

For many people the word 'grammar' conjures up school lessons in which (usually) written sentences were analysed into grammatical constituents. Grammar concerns the rules for putting words together to make sentences both in writing and in the sequences of words in spoken utterances. In sentences, some words that are closely grammatically related 'constituents' of the sentence (noun phrases, verb phrases, prepositional phrases, adverbial phrases, etc.) can often be replaced by a single alternative word. In the sentence, 'George Washington had felled the cherry tree' the noun phrase 'George Washington' can be replaced by 'he'; the verb phrase 'had felled' might remain; and the noun phrase, 'the cherry tree' might be replaced by 'it' to make the sentence 'He had felled it'.

There are rules for combining words at constituent, phrase and word levels. At the constituent level, making meaning in utterances is structured by the patterns in which we place combinations of words such as noun phrase, verb phrase and word order. The phrase level involves function words such as 'the' and 'but' respectively in the sentences '*The* horse was galloping' and 'I tried to eat *but* I was not hungry'. At the word level, making meaning is structured by inflexions such as word endings and by function words like 'by', 'with' and 'of', which can be used to indicate a meaning relationship.

Grammar is sometimes envisaged in terms of syntax and morphology. Syntax refers to the rules for making words into sentences. Morphology concerns grammatical changes to particular words. Morphemes may be 'free' or 'bound'. Free morphemes are single words ('dog', 'give') or function words ('the', 'under'). Bound morphemes are inflections attached to words ('-ly' in happi*ly*, '-ing' in 'swimm*ing*').

To develop age appropriate grammar, a child needs a good vocabulary. In development, there appears to be a sort of 'critical mass' of words that children acquire before they start to combine them into two-word utterances (Ripley and Barrett, 2008, p. 7). Where a child lacks a substantial vocabulary, he will require help developing it. It is also important to develop function words. In early language development, when children start making two-word utterances, this is taken to herald the child's awareness that putting words together has (grammatical) meaning.

Generally, until children are about 3 years old, development involves moving from single word to four-word utterances. Later children begin to use complex utterances with several clauses and phrases. Utterances begin to reflect the development of constituents, phrases, inflections and function words. Beyond the four-word stage, as utterances become increasingly complex, it becomes less satisfactory to describe or analyse utterances in terms of word count because this misses so much grammatical meaning. It is more productive to analyse the relationships of the grammatical constituents (noun phrases, verb phrases, adverbial phrases) and the development of phrase level structure.

Typically, children's grammar is seen to develop at constituent, phrase, inflection and function word levels. The utterances of children with grammatical difficulties may indicate development at the constituent level but less development at the phrase level (e.g. function word, adjective) and word level (inflections). Therefore, although the utterances tend to comprise the main information-carrying words, they sound stilted.

As children become able to grammatically connect two related ideas, compound utterances develop. Ideas might be related by similarity, difference or causation. Examples are:

- similarity ('We saw a dog *and* we saw a puppy');
- difference ('I was warm *but* mummy said she was cold');
- sequence/causation ('Jenny knocked the glass over *and* the water went all over the table').

Other compound utterances involve embedding one sentence in another ('I like the coat *that* I bought last summer'). As constituent and phrase level grammar develops, so does morphemic level grammar affecting word level relationships in utterances (words, function words and inflections). Typically, many children have acquired many early emerging morphemes (including '-ing', '-ed', 'a' and 'the') by 2½ years old (Wells, 1985).

In a basic model of receptive skills of language (Ripley and Barrett, 2008, p. 5) input comprises use, grammar, content and executive function. For receptive grammar the processes involved are processing the phonological code, analysing sentence structure and attending to tenses and morphological markers (ibid.).

Regarding output, main features are central processing, content, grammar and use. For grammar the constituent aspects are retrieving the phonological code for words, putting the words into a sentence, attending to tenses and morphological markers (Ripley and Barrett, 2008, p. 6).

Causal factors

For a small group of children, there may be a hereditary predisposition to language difficulties. This can be suggested by prevalence among other members of the family, particularly males. Physical damage to the brain through accident or viral infection may lead to severe language difficulties.

Neurological weakness, for example through birth trauma, appears to be a factor in language difficulties of some children. Fonteneau and van der Lely (2008) considered the scope of specific language disorder, estimated to affect 7 per cent of children. They examined whether it affects the general ability to segment and process language or a specific ability to compute grammar. Evidence from electrophysiological data suggested a domain-specific deficit within the grammar of language. Children identified as experiencing grammatical specific language impairment appeared to have a selective impairment only to neural circuitry that is specific to grammatical processing. They appeared to be partially compensating for their syntactic deficit by using neural circuitry associated with semantic processing.

Where material poverty or hearing impairment is associated with language difficulties they are regarded as the primary difficulty and the language difficulty is considered a secondary concomitant. In a study of preschool children from disadvantaged socio-economic backgrounds, over half were considered to have language delay. Language skills were significantly below cognitive abilities (Locke *et al.*, 2002). A child from a disadvantaged socio-economic background is also more likely to suffer illnesses leading to absences from school and have poorer nutrition than other children. Both of these factors are likely to hinder learning.

A child with a hearing impairment may be taught a sign language which has grammatical implications. A 'national' sign language may have a grammatical structure at the constituent and word order levels. Other sign languages for example the Paget-Gorman system reflect the phrase and word level grammatical structures of spoken language. Some children experience additional difficulties in developing grammatical structure.

Difficulties with syntax and morphology

As already indicated, grammar may be considered in relation to syntax (the rules for making words into sentences) and morphology (grammatical changes to particular words).

A child may show indications of grammatical difficulties at about the age of 3 years. He may have difficulties with the order of words and with making sentences of four or more words. There may be a problem with function words, so the child may use telegraphic utterances such as 'me tired' for 'I am tired' when no longer age appropriate. Key words are included but function words are often omitted.

A child, while able to formulate simple sentences, may have problems making compound ones. This may be owing to difficulties with auditory sequential memory making him unable to handle long word sequences. The child may also struggle with the grammatical relationships implicated in connecting the ideas that are complicatedly hierarchical, dependent, embedded or causal (Martin and Miller, 2003, p. 73).

The child may lack the linguistic knowledge of the rules necessary to recognise the grammatical role of words, such as the difference between nouns and verbs. For similar reasons, he may not be able to recognise the appropriate structures for verbs (van der Lely, 1994).

Short-term memory difficulties may cause problems formulating sentences. The child may have difficulties with grammatical structures because these are embedded and hierarchical. This can lead also to problems formulating sentences. The child may experience pervasive memory and organisational problems so he may require help and support with general organisation. Grammar difficulties may be a manifestation of processing difficulties relating to working memory. Accordingly, the child may be unable to make sentence structures with familiar words or use a two-noun phrase with a verb because processing demands for these are too great.

From a broader cognitive perspective, the child may have problems with auditory memory, auditory sequencing, attention and reading and writing. To the extent these contribute to grammatical development, remediating work may be undertaken. In parallel, you can more directly help the pupil improve grammatical skills and understanding.

There is a familiar tension here. What appear to be underpinning skills or abilities such as auditory memory may be weak. This might suggest working on this in a focused way. However, auditory memory has to have content and where the child has difficulties with grammar some of this should concern the development of grammatical understanding and skills. Essentially, this is an educational judgement about the extent to which underpinning skills can be improved directly and the degree to which they are likely to develop as activities using them are developed. This is a more finely focused version of judgements about the extent to which grammar can be taught as a specific skill and the degree to which it is understood when in the context of everyday utterances.

Morphology, for example prefixes (tidy/*un*tidy) and suffixes (talk/talk*ed*; cat/cats), can add grammatical information. Many children acquire a variety of these sorts of morphemes as early as 2½ years (Wells, 1985), if not expressively then receptively. Some children, however, require specific teaching and practice to learn these. Some aspects of morphology are more complex. These include changes to words that negate their meaning (stable/*un*stable) and suffixes changing the grammatical class to which the word belongs (adjective 'kind'/noun 'kind*ness*').

Where a student has difficulties with grammar at high/secondary school, he may still not understand or use complex sentences with subordinate clauses. He may continue to have problems with verb tenses, irregular plural forms and connectors (Ripley and Barrett, 2008, p. 7).

Assessment of grammar

It is clear grammar is subtle and complex. This suggests caution in applying a framework of typical development to inform the assessment of grammar difficulties. A certain variation in development and the pace of development is considered statistically normal and occurs in children without necessarily indicating the existence of difficulties. However, timely intervention implies not treating possible early indications of difficulties too lightly. Clearly there is a tension between these two positions. This requires you to make careful professional judgements supplemented with advice from colleagues and in consultation with parents. The school may decide to refer the child to a speech-language pathologist.

Assessments of the child's grammatical development are made in relation to curriculum expectations and by screening procedures and standardised assessments. The teacher might make an initial investigation.

This could involve checking the child's level of understanding of plurals, tenses, negatives, prepositions, pronouns and questions. Assessment pictures or objects might be used. For example, for prepositions the child can be asked to distinguish from two carefully designed pictures, one of which shows a ball 'in front of' a box and one which depicts a ball 'behind' the box.

Similar investigations can show whether the child understands plurals, negative and other features. If preliminary investigation suggest there might be difficulties, the school may carry out ongoing observation and monitor progress more closely. Where a teacher has concerns, she is likely to observe the child over a period of time and gather information to check early impressions. If so, the teacher may seek the views of a senior colleague and, as necessary, the advice of a speech pathologist/therapist. Even after a speech pathologist is involved the teacher's ongoing monitoring is still relevant.

Descriptive grammar may be used to inform assessment. It seeks to describe the rules that exist in a speaker's use of language and any variations of those rules. However, descriptive grammar avoids implications of correct or incorrect grammar from an imaginary vantage point outside what real speakers say and how they say it. As such, it can indicate the development of a child's grammar at different points in time, including as the child's grammar approaches the way adults usually use grammar. The descriptions can indicate the skills the child has acquired without necessarily overemphasising features not yet developed.

The 'mean length of utterance' is a popular index of grammatical complexity. One reason is that it is easy to compute. Also, in normally developing children there is a fairly linear relationship between mean length of utterance and the child's chronological age (Bishop, 1997, p. 92). Mean length of utterance involves analysing a sample of the child's spontaneous language and counting the number of morphemes in each of a number of utterances. To illustrate, 'I eat-ed a cake' comprises five morphemes. The number of morphemes in each utterance is averaged to give the mean length of utterance. Typical mean length of utterances for children of different ages is used for comparison. At age 24 months, 2 morphemes are typical. At age 40 months, 4 morphemes are usual (Martin and Miller, 2003, pp. 74–75).

More refined evaluations may bring greater precision to the assessment of specific language impairment. For example, attempts to find grammatical markers of specific language difficulty indicate that particular aspects of morphology appear to better differentiate affected and unaffected children. These aspects are marking tense and subject-verb agreement (Rice, 2000, p. 29).

As Ripley and Barrett (2008, p. 103) point out, it is possible to make a grammatical analysis by examining samples of a pupil's expressive language. Written work might also be analysed but the focus here is on utterances. Taped examples of spoken language might be analysed. The speech and language pathologist/therapist or the teacher might identify various immaturities. These could include the use of verb tenses, connectives, subordinate clauses and chosen sentence structure. They could involve the use of a range of vocabulary (ibid.).

Provision

Curriculum and assessment

The curriculum may emphasise grammar in several ways. Firstly, the overall planning may ensure sufficient time is spent on it, which is likely to be helpful for all pupils. Also, extra curriculum time may be allocated for selected pupils through various means. Small group work within a whole class setting can be used. In these groups, pupils with difficulties with grammar may spend extra time ensuring they understand and can use the grammar necessary to carry out the tasks in hand. This may be achieved through a classroom aide giving quite brief support and checking a pupil understands.

Another aspect to support grammar is to ensure it is embedded in subjects across the curriculum. Within certain subjects, there may be a particular emphasis and support for grammar. In science, curriculum planning may help ensure that the passive voice is explicitly taught and reinforced and that time is planned into lessons to ensure pupils have clearly understood the content.

Assessment may adopt small steps with regard to the development of grammar so that progress can be recognised and celebrated.

Pedagogy

Sentence recasting

Sentence recasting involves an adult responding to a child's utterance by modifying it. The adult response maintains the meaning, context, referents and main lexical items of the child's utterance. However, it modifies one or more of the sentence constituents such as subject or verb; or changes the sentence modality, for example declarative to interrogative. The recasting often corrects errors in the child's utterance. If the child says, 'He need it', the adult would recast it as 'He need**s** it' (Fey and Proctor-Williams, 2000, p. 179).

Sentence recasting is a conversational naturally occurring procedure that can be used in story reading or in everyday play. The adult does not attempt to get the child to correct his original utterance. Of course, sentence recasting is a natural part of what parents, teachers and others do. Nevertheless, children with language difficulties require more frequent recasting than other children in order to progress. Speech pathologists may teach parents and teachers the procedures which may be more successful if targeted on specific grammatical targets.

Elicited imitation

Elicited imitation is a behaviourally orientated intervention. It typically involves:

- an adult showing the child a non-verbal stimulus such as a picture;
- the adult saying an utterance related to the picture and asking the child to repeat it;
- the child trying to repeat the utterance;
- the adult rewarding a correct response (or repeating the correct utterance if the child is wrong and asking the child to try again).

Gradually the adult utterance and the reward are phased out so the child responds correctly to the picture and question only. The adult may be trying to encourage the imitation of the linking use of 'is'. She might show a picture of a black dog. The exchange might go as follows:

ADULT: Look at this picture and say, 'The dog is black'.
CHILD: Dog black.
ADULT: No. Try again. Say, 'The dog is black'.
CHILD: The dog is black.
ADULT: Well done. That's right.

A limitation of the procedure is considered to be that the adult controls the activity and the child may not be very motivated. Also the child may not generalise the learned response to less structured utterances. However, the focused nature of the activity can ensure that targeted difficulties are tackled. Furthermore modifications have been made to the procedure to help ensure that utterances are meaningful even if the task is greatly broken down. For example the adult would not begin with simply asking the child to say the word 'is' in response to a picture and build up to 'The dog is black' but begin with 'dog', then 'the dog', then 'the dog black', then 'the dog is black' (Fey and Proctor-Williams, 2000, pp. 180–83).

Modelling

Modelling is an aspect of social learning theory (Bandura, 1977, 1986). In modelling, learning takes place as the learner observes and imitates another person more accomplished at the skill or task in question. It is sometimes forgotten that modelling works best where the pupil likes and admires the person modelling the desired behaviour. (This has implications for behaviour difficulties where a child might model his behaviour on an aggressive father whom he loves but ignore the positive behaviour of a teacher or peers whom he might dislike.) Let us assume the child has a good relationship with the teacher of the classroom aide on whom he is expected to model his language behaviour.

In modelling as applied to developing grammar, typically the adult produces about 10 to 20 sentences expressing the target grammatical form. The sentences might be descriptions of pictures or responses to questions. The child listens quietly to the whole sequence. The child is then asked to respond to the same or a different set of stimuli in the way the adult had demonstrated. For example, this might involve the child trying to describe a picture. The purpose of requiring the child not to respond until the set is complete is to avoid any response interfering with the child's concentration on the forms being modelled.

Similar issues emerge in relation to modelling as arise with elicited imitation in balancing the didactic and the naturalistic. Using a varied selection of sentence recasting, elicited imitation and modelling around the same grammatical targets may optimise the strengths and mitigate against the weaknesses of the different methods.

Clear teacher communication

If the teacher communicates clearly, it can help pupils understand. Grammar is one of the aspects of language that can make understanding more difficult. Teachers' utterances may be too long, making understanding difficult. The utterances can also be grammatically complex. If they are both long and grammatically complex, greater demands are made on listeners.

The teacher can adopt whole class or small group approaches. Although these are not focused exclusively on children with grammatical difficulties, they can help all the class. Clear teacher communication is aided by avoiding long rambling utterances and numerous simultaneous instructions. Every teacher knows this makes sense but it is not so easy to remember after a long busy day. This does not necessitate the teacher becoming robotic in her language but simply being aware of clarity in expressions and requests.

On a bad day the teacher might hear herself saying, 'Just one more thing before you go out and I know I say this every lesson or at least I seem to, I know most of you listen but there are still one or two – anyway can you all – I mean all this time – put your books in your desks before you go out – and remember not to make a noise when you leave and don't all rush out at once like you did yesterday or someone is going to get hurt'. This would be more likely to be understood if it were something like, 'Listen. Please put your books in your desk now. That's it. Now this group go quietly to the door'.

Some grammatical forms are particularly difficult for pupils with difficulties understanding grammar (Ripley and Barrett, 2008, p. 16). These are:

- negation;
- passives;
- connectors.

Negation might involve asking pupils not to do something in order that they can comply with something else. You might say to pupils, 'Remember not to be distracted when you cross the road or it might not be safe'. This negation is harder to process than, 'Concentrate when you cross the road and you will be safer'.

Passives are also a more complicated form of expression than active utterances. One might say to a child, 'The book you left in the library needs to be brought back to the classroom'. It is easier to understand the same message if one were to say, 'You left a book in the library. Would you bring it to the classroom please?'

Connectors can change the meaning of an utterance. Ripley and Barrett (2008, p. 16) give a good example. 'It was raining and *then* she went out' might suggest that it had stopped raining. However, 'It was raining *so* she went out' might suggest she liked going out in the rain.

The underlying message of all this is that everyone including teachers can be clearer in the way they express themselves. Being clearer does not mean thinking about everything one says and recasting it. It involves being more aware of when we tend to be obscure. Remembering that some children find the whole area of grammar very difficult can help us to aim for simplicity and clarity in our day-to-day communications.

Resources

Among resources that may be helpful to support the development of grammar are devices that can record and play back the pupil's language in different contexts so it can be analysed by the speech pathologist/ therapist or the teacher for use in subsequent remedial work.

Therapy

Therapy may involve the speech and language pathologist working directly with pupils or working in a consultancy/monitoring role (or both). Direct work is likely to involve ensuring the pupil's vocabulary is sufficient and then encouraging the development of correct grammatical utterances through modelling and allowing practice. This will be developed and reinforced as the speech pathologist works closely with the teacher, parents and others to encourage the correct use of grammar.

Organisation

No distinctive approaches to school or classroom organisation appear essential for difficulties with grammar. However, opportunities for all pupils to develop speaking and listening are likely to benefit pupils with difficulties with grammar. Talking partners allow pupils to do this.

In a lesson the teacher may give one or two opportunities for pupils to talk with their regular talking partners to develop ideas or give their views on a topic within the lesson. If a pupil with grammar difficulties is paired with a pupil who does not have such difficulties, the former has the regular opportunity to hear correct grammar being used.

THINKING POINTS

Readers may wish to consider:

- the extent to which interventions for supporting grammar successfully balance being relatively focused but isolated and being relatively general but contextual.

KEY TEXT

Paul, R. (2007) *Language Disorders from a Developmental Perspective: Essays in Honor of Robin S. Chapman* New York, Taylor & Francis.

The essays cover a much wider area than grammar and deal with psycholinguistic contributions to the understanding of child language disorders, their nature and remediation.

Chapter 4

Communication disorders

Comprehension

INTRODUCTION

This chapter considers the nature of comprehension and how comprehension develops. I then examine difficulties with comprehension. Identification and assessment of comprehension are discussed. Provision to improve comprehension is examined with regard to the curriculum and assessment, pedagogy, resources, therapy and school and classroom organisation. The main focus is on pedagogy and the pedagogical interventions discussed: teaching for (and reminders of) giving attention, teaching listening behaviour, reducing processing demands, supporting pragmatic understanding and allowing sufficient time to respond.

The nature of comprehension and physiological processes involved

In everyday use, comprehension refers to understanding an utterance or other form of communication. Perhaps associations with the term 'comprehensive' meaning broad suggest that the understanding is clear and thorough. To say one comprehends something is usually taken to imply a fuller grasp than to say one understands something.

In the context of examining communication, comprehension may be regarded as a form of representation. In this sense, comprehension may be seen as 'a process whereby information is successfully transformed from one kind of *representation* to another' (Bishop, 1997, p. 2, italics added). A framework for analysing comprehension can be constructed involving a process ranging from sound to meaning.

When a sound is produced in proximity to an individual, the sound waves of different frequencies are channelled through the hearer's ear canal to the middle ear. This occurs for different sounds including of course those associated with speech. The sound waves reach the tympanic membrane (eardrum) between the outer and middle ear causing the membrane to vibrate at different speeds. Through mechanisms in the middle ear, these vibrations are transmitted to the 'oval window' membrane. From there, the vibrations pass to the cochlea, a spiral shaped organ in the inner ear. In the cochlea, vibrations of the basilar membrane stimulate microscopic hair cells. These cells feed impulses into the auditory nerve.

The auditory nerve along with sub-cortical systems conveys 'neurally encoded *representations*' of the frequency and intensity qualities of the sound to the auditory cortex (Bishop, 1997, p. 4, italics added). In the auditory cortex, some brain cells fire selectively in response to sounds of certain frequencies. Others respond to changes in frequency over a given range or direction.

There appears to be an intermediate level of representation between the 'neural spectrogram' of responsiveness to certain frequencies, and word recognition. Ultimately the brain interprets the stream of sounds into the discrete units of individual words. In brief then, the process of comprehending speech is one by which vibrations in the environment brought about by another person speaking are translated into neutrally encoded representations understood by the listener as words.

The development of comprehension in children and related aspects

Early phonological development may involve progression from larger to smaller units of analysis. The child at first operates on words and perhaps short phrases. He encodes them in terms of salient aspects such as the presence of phonetic features and the number of syllables (Walley, 1993). By the age of 3 or 4 years, most children seem aware of the subsyllabic units of onset and rime. Later, perhaps having been exposed to print, they recognise smaller phonetic elements. Some children aged 5 to 6 years seem unable to match or identify phonemes. As a consequence, they find difficulty learning letter-sound correspondences, but have no obvious difficulties in understanding or producing speech. This may relate to lack of one to one correspondence between segments of the acoustic signal and phonemes (Liberman *et al.*, 1989).

From the flow of speech, the child developing language identifies meaningful patterns. These are stored in long-term memory so that when heard again, they are recognised as known words. Mental representations of words have information about both the word's phonological form and its meaning. Acquiring vocabulary may be seen as storing representations of familiar speech sound sequences in a mental 'lexicon' and associating these with particular meanings. Items in the lexicon are matched with sequences of sounds in the incoming speech signal.

An incoming sentence must be parsed into phrases that correspond to units of meaning, and the relationships between these have to be decoded (Bishop, 1997, p. 11). Syntax and morphology describe this grammatical sequencing for meaning. Understanding sentences also requires the ability to use knowledge of grammar in 'real time' to interpret utterances.

Drawing on general knowledge of the world to infer meaning from a given context makes the interpretation of an utterance at all levels clearer. The understanding of longer discourse also informs interpretations. To understand an utterance it is often necessary to interpret the speaker's intentions. This is so with pragmatic aspects of communication like sarcasm and metaphor.

Comprehension difficulties

Comprehension difficulties are distinctive in some respects. Other aspects of communication than comprehension are predominantly expressive. As a result difficulties may be more apparent. Expressive speech difficulties such as stammering are clearly evident. The repetitive and obsessive aspects of speech topics and phrases that may be associated with autism are soon recognised. However, comprehension is essentially passive or receptive so difficulties with it may not be as evident. The child may not have the confidence to keep asking for clarification. For this reason, a child with comprehension difficulties can exhibit avoidance behaviour or boredom that can be misinterpreted by the teacher as uncooperativeness and naughtiness.

Difficulties with comprehension may have various sources relating to other aspects of language and communication. A child may find it difficult to maintain attention because of visual or hearing impairment. For others the nervous system may mature more slowly than typical leading to slower development of learning the skills of listening, looking and maintaining attention.

A child may find it difficult to control attention and be attracted to and distracted by non-relevant sights and sounds. Clearly, he will find it difficult to direct attention at the teacher's instructions. This might be especially so in whole class sessions. If a child has difficulty discriminating sounds, he may not receive sufficient information necessary to comprehend an utterance in the first place.

A child having difficulties understanding adult like grammar may be struggling with information storage and retrieval. This may be especially so when the sequence of an utterance does not reflect the sequence of events it conveys. The hierarchical structure of some utterances tends to make processing more difficult. Sometimes a child may have poor short-term memory. Difficulties with pragmatics (the use of communication) may extend to incorrectly interpreting others' non-verbal communication, and not understanding intention such as humour, and other non-literal expressions.

Cognitive skills may be implicated. If auditory processing is slower than typical, the child may be trying to understand one part of an utterance while the speaker is continuing with further information. The later information is therefore likely to be missed or only partially grasped. It will be evident that a clear assessment of the source of comprehension difficulties is likely to be wide ranging examining possible cognitive, sensory, emotional and other factors. Such a wide ranging assessment may well suggest the sort of interventions likely to be effective.

Identification and assessment of comprehension

As already indicated, there is the potential for the teacher and others to misconstrue attention and comprehension difficulties as bad behaviour. If a child does not understand a request, his inability to comply might be misinterpreted as defiance or uncooperativeness. Should the pupil take longer than others to respond to a teacher's question because of information processing difficulties, the teacher might incorrectly assume he has not been listening. If, on top of the child's difficulties, adults persistently misconstrue his behaviour as uncooperative, the pupil's difficulties are likely to be compounded and his frustrations increased. All this makes it important that comprehension difficulties are identified correctly and early and suitable support provided.

Such assessment may be curriculum based. That is, differences may be assessed in relation to the child's progress compared with that which is age typical in terms of the curriculum. This judgement will be informed by the teacher's knowledge of child development and variations in usual development. Where there are initial concerns, the teacher's classroom observation and recording of progress can be informed by consultation with others. The teacher might have discussions with a senior colleague and as necessary with a speech and language pathologist/therapist. Parents will be consulted to compare the child's comprehension at home.

Particular note is likely to be made of how the child responds to the language of the teacher, other adults and other children in relation to such features as the child's name being used, and requests made of him in different settings and with different people. It will be necessary to observe the child in different settings such as in class and small groups, and in various lessons of differing content, perhaps with sessions having different potential sources of interest (e.g. visual, auditory). Such observations should indicate areas of difficulty and strength. Videotaping a child in different environments, taking care to explain what is happening to the child and allaying any anxieties about the process, can provide useful analysable information.

More formal assessments include commercial tests that may be standardised for the country and the population concerned. For bilingual pupils, assessments may be developed in the pupil's first linguistic community language as well as in the national language. Assessments in both languages allow the strengths and weakness of the child's understanding (and expression) to be investigated. This should indicate whether the difficulties relate to one language or both.

Provision

Curriculum and assessment

For difficulties with comprehension, the curriculum may emphasise this aspect of communication. This can involve increasing the amount of time spent on developing the skills and understanding of comprehension. It can relate to comprehension being planned in subjects across the curriculum. Within most subjects, there may be an emphasis on and support for comprehension.

Good questioning by the teacher can reveal a pupil's level of understanding. Where pupils are able to make a judgement about how well they understand a topic, simple methods such as asking them to indicate their level of comprehension can be useful. Thumbs up may mean 'I understand everything confidently'. Thumbs level can means, 'I understand most of what is required'. Thumbs down can mean, 'I do not understand and I will need help in the next phase of the lesson'. Assessment may adopt small steps with regard to the development of comprehension so that progress can be recognised and celebrated.

Pedagogy

Teaching for (and reminders of) giving attention

Assessment information may indicate various situations and stimuli differentially capture the pupil's attention. Where this is so, such assessments may inform interventions. For example, where a pupil tends to pay better attention to visual stimuli, these may be linked to auditory ones to help attract and maintain attention. More generally, the teacher may provide visual clues such as a series of pictures to support sequences and instructions. The teacher can also name a child when giving instructions and can question the pupil to check attention. At the same time the teacher will remember that the pupil may have been attending but may still not have comprehended.

Teaching listening behaviour

For pupils with difficulties in comprehension, it may have become a habit and a coping strategy not to listen, to filter out much of what is said in the classroom. The child may lack confidence and expect not to understand, especially in certain lessons. Such habits will be difficult to modify. A good starting point will be to work on listening skills with a topic about which the pupil is interested and confident.

The pupil can be taught the prerequisites of listening. These include sitting still, looking at the speaker and watching gestures as well as listening to what is said. The teacher and teaching assistant/classroom aide can model good listening behaviour perhaps in role-play sessions. Humour can be introduced. One adult may model poor listening behaviour. The adults then ask pupils to comment on how good the adults' listening was and how it could be improved. The adults then demonstrate good listening. Next each pupil with an adult or another child practices these skills, which are monitored. Examples of good listening skills are praised by the teacher. As pupils spontaneously demonstrate good listening skills in other settings, these are encouraged too.

Useful activities for introducing and practising listening include the following (Thompson, 2003, pp. 30–3; 59–61). To help the pupil identify sounds, a recording might be used of various domestic, rural and urban sounds for the pupil to match sounds to pictures. Also the pupil can be asked to listen to various speech sounds and guess the speaker's gender, age and other features. Where the child has practised a sound (for example 's') and knows it, the teacher may encourage comprehension of the sound.

The teacher can give the child three pictures (e.g. indicating 'tea', 'sea' and 'pea'). She then asks the child to be ready to point to the picture starting with a specific sound (e.g. 's') when the teacher says the word. The teacher then screens her mouth or asks the child to cover his eyes and says the three words clearly. The pupil is expected of course to indicate the picture of 'sea'. Using this structure allows practice in listening for the initial consonant of words.

Other activities can help develop the auditory discrimination of two similar sounds (e.g. p/b, s/sk, t/d, k/g). The child is given pairs of picture cards (e.g. 'pear' and 'bear') and listens to the teacher saying one of the words. The child then indicates the corresponding picture.

To encourage listening to initial sounds, the teacher can give the child two letter cards with a related picture to provide a visual prompt. One card might show the letter/sound 'f' with a picture of a fish; the other the letter/sound 'th' with a picture of a thumb. The teacher says the word and the pupil says its initial sound.

Reducing processing demands

An example of a training programme that seeks (among other things) to help language processing and comprehension is Fast ForWord®. This programme draws on evidence suggesting two considerations are important. Firstly, language learning problems involve 'a basic processing constraint'. This concerns the rate at which incoming sensory information is 'segmented and represented'. Secondly, language learning problems are affected by aspects of morphological structures in a target language. These aspects are their frequency and 'obligatory nature' (Tallal, 2000, p. 143).

Fast ForWord® is a hierarchy of computer based training exercises that has two aims. It seeks to drive neural processing of rapidly successive acoustic stimuli to faster rates. It also aims to improve speech perception, phonological analysis and the awareness of language comprehension. It seeks these improvements through training exercises within various linguistic contexts. These exercises use speech stimuli that have been acoustically modified 'to amplify and temporarily extend the brief, rapidly successive … intrasyllabic cues' (ibid., p. 143).

More generally, the teacher may recognise a child is struggling to understand adult-like grammatical utterances, and appears to have difficulties storing and retrieving the necessary information. In such instances, the teacher might use more single phrase utterances. Where longer utterances are used, the teacher can try to make sure the sequence supports understanding. For example, it helps comprehension if requests correspond to the order in which they are to be followed. Accordingly, 'Please put on your aprons then come to the table' tends to be easier to understand than 'Before you come to the table, please put on your aprons.' A pupil having difficulties understanding the grammatical aspects of an utterance is likely to grasp key words conveying concrete meaning ('aprons', 'table').

If the context makes the meaning clear, the request is part of the usual routine and the pupil sees others complying, he is especially likely to understand. Teacher communication can aid pupils' comprehension in several ways. It should involve clear step-by-step explanations of what the pupil is expected to do and explanation of key words. It should be optimal, being neither a constant stream of words nor over-sparing. Similarly, the adult's emphasising of salient features of an utterance can help the child by reducing processing demands.

Supporting pragmatic understanding

Pragmatic aspects of language are pervasive, subtle and varied. Consequently, improving understanding is likely to be a slow long-term process. Role-play sessions or video/DVD examples can illustrate the more usual exemplars of aspects of non-verbal communication. These can then be discussed with a small group of pupils. Examples of intention can be provided and discussed. This encourages the development of aspects of communication such as humour and sarcasm. More common non-literal expressions can be explained and discussed.

There is a great leap from knowing the meaning of words and of expressions to knowing or inferring the intentions of others. This is an area that autistic pupils find difficult as will be discussed in a later chapter. Recognising situations in which a person says something but means the exact opposite is no easy matter anyway.

Allowing sufficient time to respond

In line with the limited processing capacity framework of language impairment, research has been conducted that varies different aspects of the 'input' of language to the child. Among these was an investigation of the 'wait time' in relation to discourse characteristics and verbal reasoning (Ellis Weismer and Schrader, 1993). This involved 8 to 9-year-old children with language learning difficulties. The research investigated wait time in interactions between the clinician and child using experiential (here and now) and narrative (decontextualised) tasks.

Wait time was either the naturally occurring time of about a second or a manipulated wait time of at least three seconds for the child to respond. The narrative task was the only one for which the effects of wait time was observed. For this narrative task, longer wait time improved the accuracy of responses to higher cognitive level questions tor the children with language learning difficulties. However, the longer wait time had no significant effect on lower cognitive level questions.

The teacher may allow a pupil having difficulties with comprehension extra time to respond to a question. In whole class teaching this can be done at judicious moments so as not to slow the pace of the lesson for others. In small group work and individual work it is easier. Pre-lesson tutoring may be used. It can include introducing the pupil to subject specific vocabulary such as scientific terms. Pre-lesson tutoring is used to prepare the pupil for what is to come to reduce processing demands.

Help with vocabulary

Attention and comprehension is likely to be reduced if the pupil has difficulty understanding the vocabulary that is being used in lessons. The child may get by in casual conversation with friends but find it more difficult in lessons where less familiar vocabulary is used. It is good practice in all lessons where the teacher introduces new terms that they are explained and the teacher checks pupils understand them. But more is needed than this if pupils with difficulties in comprehension are to succeed. For some pupils a brief period of the lesson with a classroom aide who can explain terms again and check the pupil understands these will help. Lists of key words with pictures beside them will aid memory.

Context is a good cue for new vocabulary. In history, the word 'ancient' might be discussed and illustrated with different very old items, perhaps museum exhibits. Various examples of sentences in which the word 'ancient' is used can be discussed. In geography, 'rain cycle' might be explained using a video segment or clear diagrams. In science, it will be necessary to carefully explain and check understanding of words that have different meanings to those in general use. Examples from science are 'force' and 'compound'.

Resources

Comprehension can be helped if the teacher uses visual aids. It is also helpful to encourage the pupil to use other sensory channels of communication to supplement the usual mode of auditory comprehension. Helping pupils to build a vocabulary for sensory modes can assist comprehension. Developing such a vocabulary provides further information about the pupil's experiences and the environment and relates it to language.

For some pupils signing boards may be used. These encourage kinaesthetic and visual memory to supplement comprehension. Communication boards and computer technology can help with comprehension. This is because they can produce the sounds of words as well as presenting the written form of the words.

Therapy

Therapy may involve the speech and language pathologist working either directly with pupils or in a consultancy or monitoring role or both. In individual sessions the speech pathologist may encourage the child's attention, listening skills and other aspects of comprehension. Through close liaison with the teacher and parents, these skills can be encouraged and applied in different contexts.

Where comprehension difficulties have been detected very late, the pupil may have experienced a considerable time in which teachers, parents and others have misinterpreted lack of comprehension as bad behaviour. In some instances this can lead to frustration, anger and emotional difficulties. Where this is the case, counselling may help by giving the pupil the opportunity to vent frustrations and find support while the core difficulty of comprehension is tackled more directly by teachers.

Organisation

For pupils with difficulties with comprehension, the teacher can signal the start of periods during which very careful listening is expected. This can be achieved simply by telling the class that they should listen and explaining that what is about to be said is important. But this can also be reinforced by having a particular place where listening is expected.

In elementary/primary schools, this is often a carpeted area where children will sit round while the teacher reads a book or tells a story. There may be an area called a reading corner or a listening corner. In high school/secondary school, the need for careful listening may be signalled by organising small group work where a classroom aide explains something to the group. In all cases it is likely that comprehension and attention will be helped if there are visual aids to reinforce what is being said.

In the wider setting of the school again listening times are signalled in periods such as school assemblies. It is important for pupils with comprehension difficulties that such periods are not too long and that attention and listening is encouraged by visual aids.

THINKING POINTS

Readers may wish to consider:

- school procedures for identifying comprehension difficulties early and ensuring they are not misconstrued as poor behaviour;
- the extent to which the teacher's communication might be improved to aid pupils understanding;
- the effectiveness of the teacher's methods of checking the comprehension of all pupils.

KEY TEXTS

Cain, K. and Oakhill, J. (Eds.) (2007) *Children's Comprehension Problems in Oral and Written Language: A Cognitive Perspective* New York, Guilford Press.

This book presents research to inform assessment strategies and interventions for children without an assessment of disabilities or disorders as well as children with specific language impairment and other conditions including autism and attention deficit hyperactivity disorder.

Paul, R. (2007) *Language Disorders from a Developmental Perspective: Essays in Honor of Robin S. Chapman* New York, Taylor & Francis.

The essays cover a much wider area than comprehension, and concern psycho-linguistic contributions to the understanding of child language disorders, their nature and remediation.

Ripley, K. and Barrett, J. (2008) *Supporting Speech, Language and Communication Needs* Los Angeles and London, Sage.

This book assumes an English context but offers a range of ideas and activities relevant for pupils with difficulties in comprehension. Chapter 2, 'Understanding Comprehension' summarises such approaches.

Chapter 5

Communication disorders
Semantics

INTRODUCTION

This chapter considers semantics, that is meaning in communication. I look at labelling, packaging and network building difficulties associated with them, difficulties with idiom, grammatical aspects of meaning and meaning relations. After touching on the assessment of semantic difficulties, the chapter sets out various aspects of provision. I outline features of the curriculum and assessment, pedagogy, resources, therapy and organisation with reference to semantics. The main focus for semantics is on pedagogy where I consider approaches to address labelling, packaging and network building difficulties, difficulties with idiom; grammatical aspects of meaning and meaning relations.

Semantics

When examining semantics in language the unit of meaning is known as the lexeme. A lexeme can be conveyed in one word or several. The word 'die' can be expressed in the single word 'expire' or in several words, for example, 'pass away' or 'meet your maker'. The same essential meaning is conveyed whether in one word or several (although the connotations of the different words and phrases can differ). For a lexeme to be meaningful the speaker requires some concept knowledge.

Generally, I need to have seen a dog and have some notion of the concept 'dog' before I can use the word meaningfully. I use the word 'generally' referring to seeing a dog and forming a concept of a dog because this is not the exclusive way a concept is formed. A blind person may not be able to see a dog but can build the concept in different ways through touch, smell and hearing. Bearing this in mind, most of the examples in what follows take the simple case that the concept relates to a physical object and that it is seen.

We say someone grasps the meaning of lexemes. In stating this, we imply that other cognitive factors support understanding of meaning. The child's memory needs to be able to link the object and the word. With such a link when the object is next seen the word will be available. Conversely, when the child next uses the word it will be with some memory of the concept and object associated with the word.

The verbal context in which the word is used also indicates that the child has grasped its meaning. A child may use the word 'cat' in an utterance bearing no apparent relationship to the usual meaning of the word. If the context does not support the word, we cannot really say that the child has understood the meaning. Aitchison (1987) suggests that in acquiring meaning, children have three basic related tasks:

- a labelling task;
- a packaging task;
- a network building task.

Each of these tasks and difficulties associated with them will now be considered.

Labelling and labelling difficulties

The labelling task involves the child discovering that sound sequences can be used as names for things. When a child starts using what seem to be early words these may not be what they appear. Apparent early words may be better regarded as 'ritual accompaniments' to a whole situation (Aitchison, 1987, p. 88). However, gradually the child broadens the circumstances under which these 'ritual accompaniments' are produced. As this occurs, we can more accurately regard the word as labelling and symbolising.

To understand the lexeme as a label is to regard it as a content word referring to an external phenomenon. This might be an object, person, action or attribute. From an early age the child interacts with parents and others who encourage linking sound with phenomena. As a result, the child comes to associate sound and phenomena. Also, from about the age of 3 years, the child seemingly endlessly asks questions about objects and other features of the environment.

This process necessitates a certain level of maturation and skill development. For example, labelling is facilitated if the child is able to do certain things or has certain notions. He needs to direct attention physically and cognitively to an object or event being named. The child requires some notion of object permanence. He needs to recognise that objects and events can be symbolised by pictures or models. Being able to label also implies word finding. This is the ability to access and retrieve words that connect with a stimulus such as a picture or item. As these skills and abilities are acquired in the course of development, the child gradually becomes more adept. He comes to increasingly establish connections that move closer to those in the adult system.

A child having difficulties with labelling may have problems with the above processes. He may have problems making sense of and storing auditory information beyond an age when this would be expected. A child may have word finding problems and may therefore make excessive use of certain expressions. He may overuse expressions lacking meaning but sustaining the utterance such as 'uh' and 'ehm'. He may make too much use of stereotyped phrases like 'sort of' or 'kind of', and filler words as in 'pass me the *thingy*'.

Packaging and packaging difficulties

In the packaging task, the child must discover which things can be packaged together under one label. A lexeme is also understood to include a package of conceptual and grammatical meaning.

Conceptual meaning may be 'underextended' as when a child can label his own dog as 'dog' but not understand the word and its meaning in connection with other dogs. Concepts may be 'overextended'. In this case the word has too wide a reference as when a child uses the word 'dog' to refer to all small animals. This is thought to relate to several factors. The child may lack knowledge. For example, he may know and correctly employ the word 'duck' but also use it for other birds, for which he does not know the correct names. The child may work from certain prototypes but may analyse them differently from adults. In such instances, the word 'star' may be used correctly but may be also used for 'spoon' because it too is shiny.

Grammatical meaning relates to the grammatical role of the word in a sentence that affects its meaning. Consider the object 'mouse' in the utterance 'The cat ate the *mouse*' and in the expression 'The *mouse* was eaten by the cat.' In these examples the grammatical meaning conveys an active and a passive role.

Difficulties with packaging are indicated if a child continues beyond the typical age to show underextended or overextended conceptual meaning. Difficulties with the grammatical meaning aspect of packaging are somewhat different. They relate to problems in understanding that the grammatical role of the word in a sentence affects the word's meaning.

Network building and network building difficulties

In the network building task, children must show how words relate to each other. Networking concerns the lexeme gaining meaning from its relationship with other words. This relationship may be that of a synonym or an antonym. It may be that the words are in the same category, as 'paper' and 'pencil' are both in the category 'stationery'.

Children tend to learn words that happen to be subordinates ('blue', 'red') before superordinates ('colour'). Word relationships include several types. They may be based on serial connection such as the months of the year. They may be homonyms, for example, 'meet' and 'meat'.

Word relationships may be homographs. The word 'wind' pronounced to rhyme with 'skinned' refers to a breeze. But 'wind' pronounced to rhyme with 'bind' refers to a turning a mechanism. Some words are polysemic. For example, 'top' can mean a spinning toy or a summit. It can mean to better someone or, in slang, to execute someone. The correct meaning is usually determined by the child using contextual cues as predictors. In discussing mountaineering, 'top' is likely to convey summit.

Similarly, different meanings are usually learned as the polysemic word appears and is taught in different contexts. Some polysemic words have a literal meaning and an abstract one. 'Soft' can mean either not very resistant when referring to a material, or over-compliant when referring to a person. Grammatical context can change the meaning of polysemic words. A phrasal verb such as 'put' can function as a pre-position in such phrases as 'put on', 'put across' and 'put away' (Martin and Miller, 2003, p. 92, paraphrased).

Difficulties with networking may occur that relate to synonyms. These arise because of the child's conceptual rigidity, the idea that one word can only mean one thing. Antonyms can be problematic for any child in that they can be relative. A mouse is 'small' compared with a 'big' elephant but 'big' beside a 'small' ant. Regarding subordinate and superordinate words, some children have difficulties recognizing the boundaries of different semantic fields. Even adults are not always sure if a tomato is a fruit or a vegetable, but leaving this aside, a child having problems with semantic fields may include common fruits in a list of common vegetables and vice versa.

Children may have difficulties with word relationships that concern serial connections such as months of the year but sequencing problems may go well beyond this. Difficulties with homonyms and homographs are likely to emerge in literacy work. With polysemic words, the child finds it hard to determine the correct meaning using contextual clues or recognising the abstract meaning of a word. For example consider a student knows the word 'top' as a spinning top. He might still not recognise that the sentence, 'The climber was near to the top' would be very unlikely to refer to a spinning top. The student may struggle to grasp that grammatical context can change the meaning of polysemic words.

Difficulties with idiom, grammatical aspects of meaning, and meaning relations

An idiom is an expression meaning more than, or something different from, the sum of the individual words of which it comprises. This applies to proverbs and sayings. Consider the proverb, 'A stitch in time saves nine'. It is difficult to see how anyone knowing only the separate literal meaning of each of the words could work out the meaning of the proverb as a whole. The same applies to sequences of words conveying an idea such as 'take away' for 'subtract'. Children learn them as chunks of meaning.

A child under 8 years old will tend to prefer to analyse each word or morphological unit in a series of words or utterances to help them with grammatical and lexical information. Older pupils and adults increasingly organise language into strings and formulaic sequences. A possible reason is that this results in quicker processing (Nippold and Martin, 1989, cited in Wray, 2001).

Idioms require a high degree of cognitive skill as well as experience to utilise the multiple referents invoked. This sort of understanding therefore develops gradually. You might suspect a difficulty if a child appears to be unable to learn idioms as chunks of meaning. It may become apparent that the child continues to regard idioms as literal sequences of individual words. This of course renders the holistic meaning inaccessible (Wray, 2001).

Regarding grammatical aspects of meaning, words can be described according to the part of speech, that is the word class they occupy in an utterance. This might be, for example, the class of noun, adjective or pronoun. However, the same word can have different grammatical functions. In the sentence, 'I bought a cat' the word 'cat' is used as a noun. In the sentence 'I closed the cat flap' the word 'cat' functions as an adjective.

As children develop language, it is as though they tend to assign to each word they use a single grammatical function. The word 'dog' may be regarded invariably as being a noun so that an expression such as 'dog basket' is not understood correctly grammatically. Similarly, the word 'green' may be expected to always be used as an adjective so that an expression such as a 'village green' is not understood grammatically. Only gradually do children learn that the same word can have different grammatical roles. Some children have difficulties with this beyond the usual age.

We can now turn to meaning relations. A sentence has a meaning structure that can remain the same even though the grammatical structure such as active or passive voice may change. Some children find it hard to retain meaning when changing from a sentence in the active voice to the passive voice. Consider the active, 'The dog chased the rabbit' and the passive, 'The rabbit was chased by the dog'. A child might on hearing the two utterances think that the second ('The rabbit was chased by the dog') meant the rabbit was chasing the dog.

This is a complex process as moving from the active to the passive voice requires the child deviate from the 'order of mention' subject-verb-object strategy. It requires the ability to utilise linguistic traces and co-referencing to assign meaning of a grammatical structure to a thematic role.

A child may have sequencing problems, for example, related to developmental verbal dyspraxia. This is a disorder in which a child has difficulty making and coordinating the exact movements that are needed to produce intelligible speech but where there is no evidence nerves or muscles are damaged. If a child has such sequencing difficulties, these are taken into account when assessing and remedying difficulties with meaning relations.

Assessment of semantic difficulties

Difficulties with meaning may be assessed according to progress made by a child in a curriculum that has developmental underpinnings. Such assessments would be informed by the professional judgement of the teacher and others in terms of typically expected development. The teacher's ongoing observation in monitoring progress is supplemented as necessary by consultation with parents, senior staff and language specialists. Collecting and analysing examples of the child's spontaneous vocabulary can be useful. It is best to sample from a variety of settings such as the home, several different subject lessons, group talk and whole class sessions. This gives a rounder picture and can help point to contexts the child might find more supportive than others.

In some assessments, the assessor points to a picture, object or activity and asks the child to name it. In order to be able to respond correctly, the child needs to be able to understand certain things. If a picture is used, the child has to understand that a picture represents something and also recognise what that 'something' is. Because the approach does not provide a context (or contextual clues) in which the word would normally be used it may not always reveal what the child knows. It is essential to know a child's level of understanding before it is assumed there are difficulties with semantic knowledge. This is because one may comprehend more than one can produce.

Where there are problems with the child's use and understanding of idiom, word elicitation tasks may be used as assessments. These show the words a child retrieves in response to word stimuli. Younger children tend to choose words that co-occur with the stimulus word co-grammatically (e.g. anticipating 'play/toys' as chunks). Older learners tend to retrieve words from the same word class as the stimulus words, anticipating 'play/work' as chunks. Idioms are particularly difficult because they occur in a conversational context adding yet another level of cognitive challenge to the task of interpreting them. Formal assessments including standardised tests are available from test suppliers.

Provision

Curriculum and assessment

For difficulties with semantics, the curriculum may provide extra time for these aspects of communication. It can also ensure that work supporting semantic development is embedded in cross-curricular planning with subjects across the curriculum. Within subjects, there may be a particular emphasis and support for semantics. Assessment may adopt small steps with regard to the development of semantics so progress can be recognised. Particular lessons in literacy for all pupils can introduce and give practice in common idioms and other aspects of meaning that children may find especially difficult.

Pedagogy

Labelling difficulties

Children having labelling difficulties may benefit from individual tutoring to help develop the necessary skills and understanding. This may include several strategies. The child will need help making links between the spoken word and the object, action or other phenomena. You will need to ensure the child's concepts are developed more securely through providing experiences such as structured experience of chairs of different shapes and sizes. Explicit teaching can be used to direct the child's attention to an object or event being labelled. Explicit teaching and extensive structured experiences can encourage the child to recognise the permanence of objects.

The child may need teaching that there are implied links between objects and events or pictures and other items (symbolisation). This can be achieved through pretend play, for example copying events such as washing, and using pictures representing objects and actions.

A child may have difficulty storing the auditory information needed to make the links for labelling. If so, he may benefit from the use of gesture or sign language. This allows auditory information to be linked with the tactile, kinaesthetic and visual features and memory. However, sign systems still require the child to have reached a level of development commensurate with understanding the symbolic nature of gesture and sign language. Graphic symbols may be used to aid labelling. For a child with poor auditory memory, such symbols provide visual clues and draw on visual memory.

A child may have a sense of symbolising through play and the use of pictures. Yet he may still struggle to learn words because of problems making sense of information and storing it. In such instances, picture matching, printed labels and sign language may be used (Martin and Reilly, 1995).

Packaging difficulties

How can a teacher help a child with underextended and overextended conceptual meaning? Firstly, you can analyse and understand the way the child perceives the problematic concepts. Then you can work on correcting misconceptions. In one to one sessions focusing on underextended concepts the adult can show the pupil other examples.

The child using 'dog' only for his own pet can be encouraged to talk about photographs, first of his own pet then of other dogs. Similar features can be pointed out extending the use of the word to other dogs perhaps beginning with dogs similar in appearance to the child's own. His dog might be small, and have short hair and a long tail so you would begin with that. Gradually you would extend the concept to less similar dogs to encourage the child to generalise the concept. The approaches for teaching vocabulary will vary depending on the child's age. For a younger child who is still extracting the rules and classifying, multiple experiential examples may be sufficient.

Conversely, a pupil having overextended conceptual meaning can be taught to particularise. In our example this involves making the necessary discriminations to distinguish small animals that are not dogs. Several photographs of dogs and of another creature such as a rabbit might be used. The pupil is asked to look for ways in which the two animals differ initially using pictures where these are unambiguous. The child might identify differences in the tail and ears of the two animals and differences in what they are eating. Other sets of photographs or video clips can be introduced once discriminations start to develop.

Difficulties with grammatical meaning in packaging may be helped in several ways. You can directly teach from exemplars. You can provide good models of the use of words in different grammatical roles. Another strategy is judiciously reshaping the child's utterances as appropriate, perhaps in time limited sessions.

Networking difficulties

Difficulties with networking relating to synonyms or antonyms can be helped by teaching them explicitly. Often this can be done as they arise in curriculum subjects. Similarly, the teacher can explicitly teach and check the child's understanding of subordinate and superordinate words and serial connections. Homonyms and homographs are likely to be taught in literacy work. You might use approaches encouraging semantic links such as Mind Maps^{TM}.

For difficulties with polysemy, the words may be taught and explained in their different subject contexts. A few words could be tackled each lesson. The meaning would be explained with reference to synonyms. For example, in science the term 'class' could be explained as 'group of substances' and in general school usage as 'group of pupils'. In this way, meaning is related to distinctive contextual clues. Particular difficulties can arise with recognising the abstract meaning of a polysemic word. This is because physical exemplars are not possible and the analogous use of the word is very subtle. Such meanings can be discussed and directly taught, beginning with a concrete example of a word. Pupils could be reminded of the usual use of the word 'sharp' referring to a knife blade or similar cutting instrument. Once this literal meaning was understood, you could move on to the use of the word 'sharp' referring to taste. It may be possible to find links between the literal and the non-concrete term. In our example, there might be a connection between the two because the taste seems concentrated just as the blade edge is narrow.

A child might know or remember only one meaning of a word and become confused if the same word is used with a different meaning. In such instances, he may be taught a synonym or antonym for the new meaning of the word. A child might know 'bill' as a request for payment but be confused by its use for part of a bird. The new meaning of 'bill' can be taught by linking it to the synonym 'beak' or the word 'beak' may be substituted. The pupil might experience difficulties understanding that grammatical context can change the meaning of polysemic words. This can be helped by direct teaching using examples and discussing them with pupils. The specific approaches will vary depending on the child's age. Clearly, explicit teaching will be different for a child aged 4 and a child aged 8 years.

Difficulties with idiom, grammatical aspects of meaning and meaning relations

Analysing the child's processing, and giving examples and explanations can help a child understand idiom. Where idiom involves using a word in a figurative sense the meanings need to be explicitly taught, explained and discussed. For example, the phrase, 'he was cold towards her' or 'she gave him the cold shoulder' should be related to the more literal meaning of cold temperature. Word elicitation tasks can provide useful information. These are used with learners experiencing difficulties with idiom and other multi-word strings. They help determine how the learner is storing and retrieving meaning through analytic and holistic processing. However, interventions need to take into account that idioms and figurative expressions are ultimately learned as holistic units.

Where there are difficulties with grammatical aspects of meaning, the teacher can try different approaches. She can explain the feature of language and give examples followed by practice and assessment. She can provide specific teaching and support to develop understanding of this feature. Approaches to teaching grammar vary according to several factors. These include the nature of the grammatical structure being taught, the child's cognitive level and the child's existing vocabulary level. Some children learn best through play or age-appropriate experience. But the direct teaching of grammar requires an existing level of symbol-structure relationship. If symbol-structure relationship is the basic problem, it needs to be established first. Not all children will develop good metalinguistic skills.

How do you help a child understand meaning relations? Practice and exemplars can help with understanding changing the grammatical structure while maintaining the meaning. Structured experience and over-learning can help the pupil maintain the meaning when hearing utterances in which grammatical structure is different to what was originally said or expected.

Resources

Among resources supporting the development of semantics are clear pictures to help with assessment and developing skills. A variety of objects are also used. These are used to assess what the pupil does and does not appear to know. Such items are also used to isolate aspects of the environment. This enables the teacher or therapist and the child to focus on the object so meaning can be conveyed and understood. Following up such work with reinforcing meaning in the day-to-day environment is also important.

Therapy

The speech and language pathologist/therapist may contribute through direct work with children or in a consultancy role or both. In one to one work, the speech pathologist will focus on semantic development. She may develop a programme in liaison with the teacher that the teacher or a classroom aide will deliver either one to one or in small group work.

Organisation

One to one work may be helpful for encouraging the development of semantics. Small group work also can enable the teacher or classroom aide to provide intensive support to help with meaning from time to time.

THINKING POINTS

Readers may wish to consider:

- with semantics, how effective the balance is between providing individual teaching and support for persistent difficulties and providing teaching for small groups and classes that support the aims of more intensive sessions;
- how every social and educational task provides an environment where the child needs to utilise semantic, pragmatic and grammatical skills.

KEY TEXT

Firth, C. and Venkatesh, K. (2001) *Semantic-Pragmatic Language Disorder* Brackley, UK, Speechmark.

This resource pack provides a framework for identifying and making provision for semantic-pragmatic disorder in children. Intended mainly for speech and language pathologists/therapists, it includes materials aimed at encouraging close working with parents and teachers.

Chapter 6

Communication disorders
Pragmatics

INTRODUCTION

This chapter explains the nature of pragmatics and then considers pragmatic difficulties. I look at the assessment of such difficultiesI go on to examine the curriculum and assessment in relation to pragmatics. The chapter explains provision. Regarding pedagogy I examine: providing basic skills and knowledge, grammatical sense in language use, social and linguistic sense, conversational skills, and helping with semantic-pragmatic difficulties. The chapter then considers resources, therapy and classroom organisation.

Pragmatics

Pragmatics is an area of linguistics that concerns the way the context in which language is used and the intention of the speaker influence its meaning. It is sometimes less specifically said to be about the use of language. Pragmatics has been said to cover 'all the ways in which grammar serves the needs of speakers as social human beings' (Foster, 1990, pp. 6–7). When listening to another person, one has to interpret what is meant in excess of the structural properties of language. In doing so, one draws on subtle skills and levels of understanding. Such skill and understanding is equally important for the speaker. Language is used for different purposes, each often requiring more than the literal content of the language used. Examples are being sarcastic, witty, ironic, polite or intimate. Pragmatics is probably one of the hardest aspects of language to master.

Pragmatic skills are necessary in different contexts (Anderson-Wood and Smith, 1997, pp. 40–1). Depending on their culture and subculture, people may have different ideas of what constitutes politeness and rudeness. A child or young person may be insufficiently aware of these notions, taking account of his age. If so those with whom he communicates are likely to perceive him as impolite. A child may find it easier to communicate in certain situations such as the home, school or a youth group than others. This may be because he feels more at ease in some situations than others. Also, in some situations, the topics may be more accessible and understanding may be shared.

It tends to be easier to talk about current activities than past ones. This is partly because with current activities objects and circumstances are visible at the time of speaking providing a supportive context. Communication is likely to differ according to the role of the speaker. If the speaker is communicating with an equal, then communication is likely to be different from a situation in which the speaker is conversing with someone in authority. Where a child with pragmatic difficulties does not grasp this, it is likely to affect the response of the person he is addressing. This in turn will affect the child.

One tends to communicate differently with people depending on the relationship, for example how familiar one is with them. This is because the history of the relationship of someone well known to us provides reference points for communication not possible with comparative strangers. Even adults who otherwise communicate well seem to sometimes forget this. Someone you have just met at a social gathering might talk to you about 'Jane and her friend Robert' as if you should know who they are when you cannot possibly know.

As well as being affected by past knowledge of the person to whom we are speaking, communication is also influenced by the current state of a relationship. If you are on friendly terms with your communication partner, it affects communication. The knowledge of the partner with whom one is communicating, such as their perceived emotional state and their knowledge, influences communication. The topic of a person's communication is influential; for example whether one is ignorant or knowledgeable about it.

The linguistic context refers to what has gone before in the communication and how we responded to it. This implies that for communication to go smoothly, what is said must fit a preceding pattern. Also implied is a sense of communicative direction. This is a predictable structure to longer stretches of communication. Inferential context refers to what one infers from what is said beyond the literal word meaning. It involves indicating that one has understood the communicative partner's apparent intention as well as the literal words spoken. This implies considering the significance of what has been said by both people.

When you consider the range of pragmatic factors their complexity becomes apparent. To be able to use language effectively, it is necessary to have sophisticated understanding of the social context. This includes insights into what the person with whom you are communicating is and is not likely to know. This level of understanding of others naturally takes time to develop and refine. Where there are difficulties in this area the teacher needs to be both patient and perceptive in order to provide effective support.

Pragmatic difficulties

The American Speech-Language-Hearing Association (www.asha.org) suggests pragmatics involves three major skills. The first concerns using language for different purposes, such as for a greeting. The second skill involves changing language according to the needs of the listener or situation, for example speaking differently to an adult than to a baby. The third skill is following the rules of conversation or story telling, for example keeping to the topic.

Accordingly, American Speech-Language-Hearing Association indicates that individuals having difficulties with pragmatics may say things in conversations that are unrelated or inappropriate, tell stories in a disorganised way and use little variety in language.

Pragmatic difficulties may affect both expressive and receptive pragmatic abilities. Children with pragmatic difficulties have primary difficulties with communication and conversation. But they do not necessarily have the behaviours associated with autism or difficulties with other aspects of language such as grammar.

There is debate about how the difficulties of children with pragmatic problems might be 'positioned' in relation to other disorders. Pragmatic difficulties can be seen as having predominantly features of autistic spectrum disorder. They can be considered as having mainly features of specific language disorder. They can be seen as being between the two classifications (Bishop, 2000, pp. 99–113). There is a developmental range. The boundaries of acceptability of the pragmatic behaviour of a 4-year-old will be different to that of a 14-year-old, especially in the social and linguistic sense.

Difficulties with basic skills and knowledge

Turn taking is a necessary skill that preceds pragmatic skills. Early turn taking begins in infancy with parent-child games and simple parent-child bonding activities. There are a range of basic skills associated with pragmatics. These include the developing ability and motivation to interact. In such interaction another person might do the initiating or the child might participate in an activity such as singing a song. Sharing attention is important.

Where a child has difficulties with such basic skills and knowledge, this is associated with pragmatics difficulties.

Difficulties with grammatical sense in language use

An individual achieves grammatical cohesion in utterances in several ways. Utterances may be linked to one another to avoid unnecessary repetition; may draw on shared assumptions and understanding; and are likely to keep the listener's interest. This cohesion is achieved through such means as:

- reference;
- substitutions [SC1] conjunctions.

In reference, grammatical short forms are used, for example to carry over meaning from earlier utterances. An example is when recurring words or phrases are replaced by a pronoun. In substitution, a synonymous word or phrase stands in place of an already used word. This is the case in the utterance, 'I bought a *calculator and compass* but I've lost the *equipment*'. Conjunctions join utterances to avoid repetition. We may wish to avoid saying 'Robert went to the shops. Robert went to the post office. Robert went to the cinema'. Instead, we say, 'Robert went to the shops, the post office and the cinema'.

Difficulties are evident where a child is unable to use such devices. The marking of new information is relevant. For example, if one says 'I saw a car' this does not suggest new information. However, to say 'I saw the car' does indicate novel information. Also relevant is providing references before using pronouns. If one says 'Jenny told her sister that *she* was going to be late' there is ambiguity. It is unclear whether 'she' refers to Jenny or her sister. It would be clearer to say (if this was intended), 'Jenny told her sister that she, Jenny, was going to be late'.

Difficulties with social and linguistic sense

Several important features enable utterances to make social and linguistic sense. Speaker's intention relates to speaking for a purpose such as asking a question or making a criticism. Shared understanding of the context of an utterance concerns the speaker and listener understanding with whom they are communicating.

Inference and implication involve the speakers and listeners understanding and being able to respond suitably to various conventions. One such convention is a polite, indirect request. To understand someone at a dining table asking, 'Is there any salt down there?' you need to realise they are probably implying, 'Pass the salt please'. Where a pupil has difficulties in these areas, he may respond inappropriately to utterances and struggle to maintain meaningful exchanges.

Difficulties with conversational skills

As has already been indicated, conversational skills involve being able to use suitable grammatical forms to convey information through such devices as reference, substitutions and conjunctions. Conversation involves various abilities. If a child or young person has difficulties with these, they are likely to impair conversational skills.

It may indicate difficulties relating to topic in conversation if a pupil tends to change topic excessively, or appears restless. Or the child might, in response to a topic being initiated by another person, respond tersely. He might be disinclined to extend the topic or introduce a new one. The pupil may not understand the signals conveying that a topic is being introduced. A child having difficulties with turn taking in conversation may interrupt or fail to pick up signals that the other person wants a turn. Where a child has not learned to adapt forms of address to different situations and people, his speech can be condescending to adults or overly formal towards other children.

A child may have difficulty recognising that a conversation is breaking down because of misunderstandings or interruptions. He may have difficulty repairing the conversation. An important element here is the marking of new and old information and presupposition skills. Where the child contributes to the breakdown of the conversation, he may not realise.

Difficulties may be experienced with conversations where what is being discussed is not in the here and now. Other difficult aspects are reference to emotional states, hypothetical situations or causal links. In non-verbal communication there may be various problems. The pupil may be unable to use suitable facial expressions. He may not be able to follow expectations of bodily proximity, for example standing uncomfortably close to someone. He may find it hard to use gestures appropriately or to match body language and verbal language.

Semantic-pragmatic difficulties

As we saw in the chapter concerning semantics, for a lexeme to be meaningful, a speaker has to have a certain amount of knowledge of concepts. Also, to grasp the meaning of lexemes implies that other cognitive factors support the understanding of meaning. The context of word use is also an indication the child has grasped its meaning. Semantic-pragmatic issues therefore concern the interaction of pragmatic and semantic skills and knowledge.

Semantic-pragmatic difficulties concern both meaning and use of language. The term 'semantic-pragmatic disorder' describes a developmental disorder of language meaning and function. It is debated whether semantic-pragmatic disorder should be considered separately from autistic spectrum disorder (Gagnon *et al.*, 1997).

Children considered to experience semantic-pragmatic disorder may be overly literal in their attempts to make inferences. They may have a primary difficulty with semantic knowledge and may have difficulties with grammar. These children have problems with word finding, learning vocabulary and auditory comprehension. Their poor socialising skills restrict socialising with peers.

Assessment

There are a number of possible causal factors of pragmatic difficulties. These include semantic difficulties. Cognition may be impaired. Imagination may be limited. Institutionalisation or adverse environmental influences are other factors. The child may lack social experience influencing the development of appropriate styles of interaction. Certain neurological conditions may be implicated (Anderson-Wood and Smith, 1997, p. 32 paraphrased).

The child's progress in the curriculum can inform an assessment of difficulties. If such an assessment indicated problems, the teacher would take further advice as necessary. Where there are concerns, you might assess conversational skills. You make a baseline assessment by observing and recording conversational skills in different contexts. An audio or video recording may be made. A video recording has the advantage that it allows the social setting to be seen and non-verbal communication to be assessed. Assessment in different contexts is more informative that assessment in one situation because communication may vary in different settings (Stacey, 1994). If you repeat the process at agreed intervals, you will be able to monitor progress. Commercial tests, checklists and profiles are also available.

In assessing pragmatic problems, it is also important to ensure basic auditory comprehension skills are at age-typical levels. A child with impaired comprehension may display inappropriate responses, but these may signify a problem with reception rather than with social appropriateness.

Consider a bilingual child brought up in a linguistic minority community. He may learn the home language first and the language of the wider community (say English) later, perhaps beginning at school. In such circumstances, the child will tend to develop the skills of communication associated with his first language. These may be interpreted as difficulties in the English-speaking context.

For example, it may be acceptable that a child responds minimally in his first language community. This may be interpreted as a potential communication difficulty in school. In this instance, you may need to liaise with specialist teachers supporting the child's learning of English. What if it appears there are pragmatic difficulties? In these circumstances the child's communication will be assessed in different contexts including different situations but also different linguistic communities.

There is debate about the balance of approach in this area. On the one hand, the teacher will want to encourage and respect cultural differences. On the other hand, you will want to teach and encourage the linguistic/pragmatic patterns of the predominant language of the country. Of course, speaking English (or whatever is the wider community language) as an additional language is a language difference not a language disorder. However, there remains the question of what should and should not be 'corrected' to help ensure communication is understood.

Provision

Curriculum and assessment

For difficulties with pragmatics, the curriculum may provide extra time for these aspects of communication. It can also ensure that work supporting pragmatic development is embedded in cross-curricular planning with subjects across the curriculum. Within subjects, there may be a particular emphasis and support for pragmatics.

A pupil may have difficulty with conversational abstractions. If so, although all aspects of the curriculum are implicated, it may be more apparent in some subjects than others. Consequently, teachers of geography where the topic is not about the present environment may require careful support. In history topics concern distant times and create additional complications. The planning of these subjects can include activities to help ensure the child with pragmatic problems has practice in using potentially difficult expressions correctly.

Assessment may adopt small steps with regard to the development of pragmatics so progress can be recognised.

Pedagogy

Providing basic skills and knowledge

There are several interventions for developing basic pragmatic skills and knowledge. You may use interactive activities such as peek-a-boo and rhymes and songs with repeated sounds and movements. Also used are communication facilitation techniques. These aim to be very responsive to the child's communicative attempts. They encourage the adult to attend less to the child's speech performance and more to the child's interests and preferred activities. Techniques to facilitate communication can be used at different levels.

These techniques may be employed at a pre-linguistic level, for example attention sharing. Communication facilitation techniques can be used at the linguistic stage, for example repeating what the pupil says. They can be used at the complex language stage, for example making a statement that is likely to lead the child to say something. Furthermore, naturalistic interventions include the aspect of 'contingent responding' (Anderson-Wood and Smith, 1997, p. 85). This involves sensitively and alertly responding to what the child says or indicates.

Grammatical sense in language use

For difficulties involving grammatical sense in language use, the speech and language pathologist/therapist may work with the child directly. The teacher and speech pathologist will also liaise and the teacher will take opportunities to reinforce and develop grammatical sense. The aim is to provide models of grammatical cohesion devices and help the child practise them. The practice may involve the use of role-play.

Where the child makes mistakes these can be selectively reinterpreted back to the child. This enables the pupil to hear the correct formulation without feeling that he is forever getting things wrong.

Social and linguistic sense

Interventions to help with social and linguistic sense include being taught possible signals of the speaker's intentions and given examples of implication and inference. Opportunities to use similar signals can be provided in role-play and encouraged when they appear in day-to-day communication.

Opportunities can be used that arise appropriately during the day. Consider the use of greetings. Perhaps the child tends not to use greetings but tends to go straight into conversations with someone he does not know. Firstly greetings can be regularly practised with the class or a small group. Pupils can greet the teacher or a conversation partner in the morning and in the afternoon routinely. Then in role-play sessions, the pupil can use greetings once told the time of day it is supposed to be (morning, afternoon, evening). Next, when there are visitors to the school, the pupil might be asked to welcome them, remembering to greet them appropriately. As the pupil learns to use greetings correctly in ad hoc occasions as they arise, he is praised.

A pupil may have difficulty finding the correct form of address for speaking to a child or to an adult. He may speak too familiarly with an adult or use language with a child that the child could not be expected to understand. Videotaped extracts of children's language can be played and studied so that the pupil can be shown the sort of language the child of a younger age uses. The examples might be of children several years younger than the pupil.

The pupil might then be given a task in role-play with a partner to explain something as if it were to the child whose language had been studied. The teacher will praise the pupil's efforts when they are responsive to the supposed listener and perhaps offer alternatives where the communication is not so well pitched. The pupil can be given opportunities to put the skills into practice by perhaps working with younger children for a session in which he helps and explains things to them. A similar approach can be taken to develop suitable language aimed at an adult speaking partner.

It can be very difficult to recognise the social use of persuasiveness. A game can be played to encourage the use of indirect ways of trying to influence someone else. The teacher and the teaching aide might role-play a few examples first to show what is expected. Then the pupils are grouped in pairs. One is told what he should try to get his partner to do but is asked to try to achieve this by indirect means. Let us say one pupil is seated on a chair while the other stands. The aim for the standing pupil is to get the conversation partner to give up his seat without asking directly. He might say, 'I am feeling a little tired' or 'Is that seat comfortable? I wish I were able to sit down for a few minutes'.

The pupil with pragmatic difficulties is likely to need extra sessions along these lines to really develop the skills confidently. He can play the part of the person trying to persuade as well the listener. Where he plays the role of the listener, he can be asked what it was that he thought the conversation partner was trying to achieve. This will help the receptive understanding of pragmatic skills as well as the expressive ones.

An example of an intervention to assess and encourage social language is the *Social Use of Language Programme* (Rinaldi, 2001). This is intended to help develop language skills in real life settings. It teaches the student basic social communication skills and an awareness of his own role and that of others in communication.

Conversational skills

A child may have difficulty with a conversational topic because he does not understand signals that the topic is being introduced. The child can be taught to recognise common opening gambits of an intention to start a new topic and respond accordingly. For example, you may teach the use of open ended questions such as, 'What did you think of the movie last night?'

The response to this may involve asking a question ('You mean the horror movie?') or commenting from his experience ('It was good but not as good as *Dracula*').

What if the child does not recognise when someone is trying to round off a conversation and has difficulty signalling that he wants to do so himself? In such instances, he can be taught to listen for possible signals that someone would like to change topic. They might say something like, 'I liked the school trip too, but I haven't told you about my friend's visit'. The pupil can learn and practise more subtle ways of indicating a desire to change topic himself.

A child having difficulties with turn taking can be taught the signals that the other person wants a turn. This might be a pause or question. The pupil will also need to be taught to respond to such signals and how to use such signals himself. Role-play and encouragement when such devices appear in everyday conversation can help. The child may not have learned the correct forms of address for different situations and people. If so, you can point this out as it arises. Where it can be done in an encouraging way you can explain why the original form is not suitable while providing examples of more apt forms.

Should the child find it hard to recognise that conversation is breaking down and have difficulty repairing it; you can teach the signs of conversation breakdown. Also the skills for repairing it can be taught and practisced. For example, the child might be taught how to ask clarifying questions. Where the child contributes to conversational breakdown without realising, you can signal the breakdown. For example, you can simply say you do not understand or you can employ a clarifying question or other repair strategy.

Helping a pupil having difficulty with conversational abstractions has implications for all aspects of the curriculum. However, it may be more apparent in certain subjects. Geography topics deal with 'now' but not with 'here'; history topics concern 'here' but not 'now'. Where the child has a difficulty with conversations involving abstractions, specific support may help for some subjects such as pre-teaching some concepts.

Help with non-verbal communication will take account of its culturally variable nature. The teacher or others may model suitable non-verbal communication. You can help the child practise non-verbal communication through role-play. You can encourage and praise suitable approximations as the child shows them in day-to-day communication.

Helping with semantic-pragmatic difficulties

It is important that pupils with semantic-pragmatic difficulties receive help with communication interaction skills in the early years and at school. Support in the family is also important. Assessment could indicate that, centrally, semantic difficulties lead to and compound the pragmatic difficulties. In such a case, interventions may include those intended to improve semantic skills. You can help the child develop phonological awareness skills through over-learning and practice.

Resources

In assessing pupils for pragmatic difficulties, an audio or video recorder may be used. Commercial tests, checklists and profiles are also used and details of these can be obtained for any of the well-known test suppliers. To help develop pragmatics, specific programmes may be used, for examples ones intended to help with social language.

Therapy

The speech and language pathologist may work directly with children. She may also work in a consultancy role perhaps assessing the child, initiating some early interventions and then liaising with the teacher to develop fuller scale programmes.

Organisation

Classroom organisation to help pupils with the development of pragmatics includes opportunities to work individually from time to time with the teacher or a classroom aide. You may provide opportunities for role-play to teach and practise pragmatic skills.

THINKING POINTS

Readers may wish to consider:

- how the teacher and speech and language pathologist/therapist can determine the combinations of approaches (direct teaching, modelling, role-play and encouragement of skills in day-to-day communication) that work best with particular children;
- how every social and educational task provides an environment where the child needs to utilise semantic, pragmatic and grammatical skills.

KEY TEXTS

Firth, C. and Venkatesh, K. (2001) *Semantic-Pragmatic Language Disorder* Brackley, UK, Speechmark.

This resource pack provides a framework for identifying and making provision for semantic-pragmatic disorder in children. Intended mainly for speech and language pathologists/therapists, it includes materials aimed at encouraging close working with parents and teachers.

MacKay, G. and Anderson, C. (Eds.) (2000) *Teaching Children with Pragmatic Difficulties of Communication: Classroom Approaches* London, David Fulton Publishers.

Chapters include: 'Action and interaction: the roots of pragmatic communication'; 'Pragmatic communication difficulties'; 'Primary age pupils with pragmatic difficulties' and 'The school as an integrated support system for pupils with pragmatic difficulties'.

Chapter 7

Autism

INTRODUCTION

This chapter describes autism and explains its prevalence, causal factors and identification and assessment. Turning to provision, I consider curriculum and assessment, pedagogy, resources, therapy, organisation and other aspects.

Autism

Autism, first clinically identified by Kanner (1943) involves a 'triad' of impairments (Wing and Gould, 1979): social isolation, communication difficulties and insistence on sameness.

Clinical guidance (American Psychiatric Association, 2000, pp. 51–3) specifies the disorder must manifest itself before the age of 3 years, and defines it in relation to: social difficulties, communication impairment and restricted behaviours.

The diagnostic criteria concerning social interaction are: 'marked impairment in the use of multiple non-verbal behaviours…; failure to develop peer relationships appropriate to developmental level; a lack of spontaneous seeking to share enjoyment, interests, or achievement with other people…; lack of emotional reciprocity' (ibid. p. 75). At least two of these elements must be manifested.

Regarding communication and language, impairments are manifested by at least one of the following (ibid. p. 75): 'delay in, or total lack of, the development of spoken language…; in individuals with adequate speech, marked impairment in the ability to initiate or sustain a conversation with others; stereotyped and repetitive use of language or idiosyncratic language; lack of varied, spontaneous make-believe play or social imitative play appropriate to the developmental level'. A third to a half of autistic children do not develop speech (Prizant and Wetherby, 1993) and may use alternative communication such as picture symbols, assistive technology devices or signing.

Regarding thinking and behaving flexibly a child with autistic disorder shows 'restricted repetitive and stereotyped patterns of behaviour, interests and activities' (American Psychiatric Association, 2000, p. 75).

Adults with autistic spectrum disorder may be oversensitive to certain sensory stimuli (Lawson, 1998). Some children seem undersensitive to certain stimuli. About a third of children with autism may have epilepsy (Volkmar and Nelson, 1990). Only about 5 to 17 per cent are later able to live a normal social life and have a vocation (Gillberg and Coleman, 2000). If a child has a non-verbal intelligence quotient within the age typical range and has some functional language skills by the age of 5 years, the prognosis is better. In any event progress can be made especially if parents, teachers and others work closely together.

Prevalence of autism

The ratio of males to females with autism is around 4:1; or where there are learning difficulties 5:1 (Lord and Schopler, 1987). In the 1990s, the prevalence of autism was estimated as 7 to 17 per 10,000 children in both rural and urban settings (Gillberg et al., 1991). More recently, autism is thought to affect 10 to 30 children in every 10,000, although the rate for the population that includes older children and adults is thought to be higher.

Prevalence for the broader category of autistic spectrum disorder, which includes autism and other syndromes, is thought to be about 60 in every 10,000 children under the age of 8 years (Medical Research Council, 2001). The apparent increase in the prevalence of autism may be real or an artefact of changes in clinical and administrative diagnostic practices.

Causes

There is 'overwhelming evidence' autism has a biological basis and a strong genetic component (Medical Research Council, 2001, p. 21). Autism may have several causes affecting the same brain systems. Several genes may act with environmental factors to lead to autism (Rutter, 1996). The International Molecular Genetic Study of Autism Consortium (1998) first identified the location of a few susceptibility genes that might be involved in the causation of autism (genes 2, 7, 16, 17 have been considered). The Autism Genome Project (www.autismspeaks.org/naar-launches-largest-autism-genetics-study) continues such research.

Evidence indicates vaccines are 'not associated with autism' (www. cdc.gov). Among possible environmental factors are: illness during pregnancy, childhood illness, food intolerance and reaction to pollutants. The interaction between such possible elements and proposed genetic and biological factors appears influential.

People with autism may have a limited 'theory of mind', having particular difficulties recognising and interpreting the emotional and mental states of others, leading to social and communication difficulties (Baron-Cohen, 2000). A joint attention deficit in a child with autism may impair the child's capacity to focus on something that is capturing the attention of other people. This deficit may lead to the child preferring non-social events such as using a computer to social events. This in turn will tend to impair language, social communication and the child's theory of mind (Mundy and Neale, 2001). Executive dysfunction may affect ability to: plan actions, disengage from the external context, restrain unwanted responses, maintain a cognitive focus and remain on task and monitor one's performance (Ozonoff, 1997).

Identification and assessment

Early identification and assessment undertaken by various professionals is important. A multi-disciplinary assessment draws on the perspectives of parents, teachers and others over an extended period of time. Some local authorities designate professionals with specialist knowledge of autism. Initial broad screening instruments are commercially available.

Thorough diagnosis combines systematic observations of the child at home and/or in other settings, and an account of the child's history from birth to the time of the assessment. Diagnostic instruments use interviews, ratings and structured observations. One assessment (Lord et al., 2000) uses the observation of semi-structured activities for individuals from preschool to adulthood; another (Wing et al., 2002) employs a semi-structured interview with parents. Further sources of information for diagnostic assessment include information from the child, parents and other family members, and discussions with professionals who know the child well.

Provision

Curriculum and assessment

The curriculum should be developmentally suitable and chronologically appropriate and is likely to emphasise communication, social skills and play as well as academic skills training. Particular methods of teaching and learning enable these aspects of curriculum content to be made meaningful and tolerable to the child. The curriculum incorporates the special interests of the autistic child to increase motivation, success and time spent on task.

Curriculum based assessments are interpreted with care and draw on professional knowledge and understanding of autism as 'correct' responses may not always reflect a pupil's understanding. Facility in the mechanics of reading may conceal poor understanding of the content and its nuances.

Pedagogy

Pedagogy may involve repeated brief structured learning sessions, drawing on behavioural and cognitive approaches and focusing on sensitively building social interaction and communication skills. Simpson (2005) identifies evidence based practices.

'Structured teaching'

Division TEACCH (www.teacch.com) is a programme for autistic people and their families (Schopler, 1997). Its structured teaching approach involves organising the classroom to reduce visual and auditory distractions (Mezibov and Howley, 2003, p. 8). This helps the child focus and ensures teaching process and styles are suitable. Visual information helps intelligibility and encourages learning and independence. Structured teaching aims to 'increase independence and to manage behaviour' by considering autistic individuals' 'cognitive skills, needs and interests' and adjusting the environment as required (ibid., p. 9). It involves physical structures, daily schedules, work systems and visual structure and information.

Physical structure and organisation concern arranging furniture, materials and general surroundings to add meaning and context to the environment. The child may have a workstation, an area may be screened to reduce distractions and different colours may be used to designate an area for different activities. Daily schedules may include visual timetables and diaries, using writing, pictures, drawings or representative objects. These help the pupil organise changes in place or activity. Presenting a transition object can indicate what the child should do next (a compact disc indicating a computer lesson). Alternatives offered in schedules encourage pupils to make choices and decisions.

Work systems, presented visually, aid the pupil completing specific activities. Work can be placed on a tray on the pupil's left and when completed transferred to a 'finished' tray on the right. For higher attaining pupils, work systems can be written. Visual structure and information concerning specific tasks and activities involve visual clarity (e.g. colour coding), visual organisation (e.g. using organising containers) and visual instructions (e.g. written or pictorial cues).

Lovaas Programme

The Lovaas Programme, based on the principles of applied behavioural analysis, uses behavioural methods to teach skills and reduce unwanted behaviour (Lovaas, 1987; and www.lovaas.com). It aims to decrease behaviours considered in excess, such as obsessive behaviours, and decrease those considered in deficit, such as communication and social skills.

Usually, the child is taught individually at home by a therapist trained to use the programme, and by the child's parents and volunteers. Ideally, the programme should commence before the child is 42 months old. Teaching occupies 10–15 minute sessions, followed by a period of play, followed by a further work session. Normally, the child sits opposite the therapist at a table and instructions are given with physical prompts as necessary. Required responses are rewarded and unwanted responses ignored or given time out.

Target behaviours are specified (e.g. repeating a word) and a sequence or 'drill' presented to teach the target behaviour. The first three goals, 'come here', 'sit down' and 'look at me' are followed by work such as imitation, matching, labelling objects and pre-school academic skills.

Discrete trial teaching/training

Discrete trial training (DTT) (Committee on Educational Interventions for Children with Autism, 2001) is a structured, therapist led intervention. It involves breaking behaviour into smaller parts, teaching one sub-skill at a time, shaping required behaviours until they are securely learned and prompt fading. Reinforcement is directly related to the task. DTT comprises:

- an adult *presentation* (an environmental cue or instruction cuing the child to carry out the required behaviour);
- the child's *response* to the cue;
- the *consequence* following the child's response (reward for a correct response);
- a brief *pause* following the consequence and preceding the next instruction.

If your presentation does not have the desired effect, you may prompt the child or model the action required. DTT may involve intensive regular work sessions of individual instruction several times a day. This may build from brief sessions to longer ones of perhaps several hours each day over many months. Programme content can vary. For example, DTT is used in the Lovaas Programme beginning with early receptive language and leading to skill programmes in self-help, in the school and in the community. Other DTT programmes follow different curricula.

Consider teaching a 'readiness' skill such as sitting on a chair. You provide the stimulus to cue the required behaviour perhaps using a request or signal. The correct response is for the child to sit on the chair. He is then rewarded. There is then a brief pause before the next instruction. The skill might be further broken down into steps such as approaching the chair, and standing near it. Each step is taught using the same approach. The child is rewarded initially even when he needs guiding, begins to comply or tries. DTT programmes require considerable commitment. Therefore care is taken to evaluate and monitor effectiveness for each child, the effort required by the family and others and whether it is sustainable. See the Indiana Resource Centre for Autism (www.iidc.indiana.edu/irca/behavior/discretetrl.html).

Pivotal response training

Pivotal response training aims to improve the social-emotional and communicative behaviour of autistic children about 3 to 10 years old. It is a naturalistic intervention targeting pivotal areas of a child's functioning likely to lead to broader changes in other non-targeted behaviours. Procedures structure the environment to teach these pivotal skills so broader areas of social and communicative functioning are improved (Koegel and Koegel, 1995).

Two pivotal areas for autistic children are motivation and responsiveness to multiple cues. You may seek to increase a child's motivation to learn new skills and to initiate social contacts and respond to others doing so. You may further increase motivation through turn taking, giving the child choices and reinforcing attempts. This aims to enable the child to respond to opportunities to learn and interact that arise day to day. Pivotal response training uses Applied Behaviour Analysis involving positive child centred and family centred procedures. It may involve short sessions (10 minutes to 1 hour) several times a week. It includes using:

- varied tasks encompassing mastered and novel activities;
- modelling required behaviour such as turn taking;

- naturally occurring reinforcers such as responding meaningfully to a child's requests (e.g. helping a child obtain a drink when a drink is requested)
- the child's preferred activities and allowing choices within them.

Such procedures are incorporated into day-to-day teaching and learning opportunities in natural settings. Asking questions, giving instructions and giving the child opportunities to respond should all be clear, uninterrupted and task appropriate. A review concludes pivotal response training is effective and that such approaches in educational settings can 'optimise communicative and social-emotional functioning' (Humphries, 2003, p. 5). (See www.researchintopractice.info.)

Sensory integration

The theory for sensory integration was developed by an occupational therapist. An autistic individual appears to have difficulty processing information received through the senses. This may relate to: processing speed, how information is interpreted and how memory functions in relating current information to previous experiences. Some behaviour associated with autism such as hand flapping and walking on tiptoe may relate to dysfunctions of sensory integration.

Sensory integration therefore aims to reduce sensory disturbances connected with touch, movement and sense of position and involves the tactile, proprioceptive and vestibular senses.

For problems with tactile sensitivity a soft surgical brush may be used to and brush the arms, legs and back. Interspersed with this the occupational therapist manually pushes together the joints of the elbows, knees and arm and hip sockets (joint compression). For proprioceptive problems joint compression and jumping on a small trampoline may help. For vestibular problems balancing exercises, activities involving the hand and arm crossing the body mid line and work with an occupational therapist to strengthen muscle tone may be employed (Case-Smith and Bryant, 1999).

The Picture Exchange Communication System

The Picture Exchange Communication System (Bondy and Frost, 1994) aims to help children using pictures to request things from others and for other purposes (www.pecs.org.uk). The child 'exchanges' a picture or symbol representing, for example, an item or activity for the thing they would like. Single things are taught initially, such as 'drink'. In early stages you should avoid pre-empting the child's attempts to communicate by volunteering for him the anticipated communication, but wait for the child to hand over the picture conveying the request. Later the child is taught to construct sentences and to use pictures to offer comments.

The Children's Talk Project

The Children's Talk Project is an evidence based communication programme for autistic children. Parents receive consultation and training in particular parent-child communication skills (Aldred *et al.*, 2004). To help a child's capacity for social referencing, parents are shown how to improve parent-child joint attention. They are trained to provide a supportive commentary on their child's behaviour. Parents are also trained to show their child how language can be used to work for them by translating his non-verbal communication into simple words.

They also learn how to use language scripts in particular contexts to convey certain meanings and intentions, so helping their child's understanding. Parents and pre-school children attend monthly sessions for six months and for a further six months attend sessions less often. Having been coached in communication skills using video feedback, parents are asked to plan daily half hour sessions to coach their child in the development of these skills.

Joint action routines

Joint action routines (Prizant *et al.*, 2000) use day-to-day routines that encourage communication, for example food preparation. For making a sandwich, you might lay out ingredients but require the child to request each one (bread, butter, ham). It should be made clear who does what. The child might request items then spread the butter or he might spread the butter and place the slice of ham on the bread. In different activities the allocation of roles and activities may differ. The activity will involve clear discrete parts and a clear sequence.

Initially you will establish the routine rather than request responses from the child. You may demonstrate what to do (modelling) then get across the expectation that the child will do part of the routine, conveying turn taking. To encourage communication you might pause in the routine and say what you want the child to say (e.g. 'butter'). Should the child say the word, the activity continues. If the child does not respond, you can try several more times before modelling the required response and continuing with the activity. This structure can encourage use of the Picture Exchange Communication System, gestures or manual sign language.

Once the routine is established and the child knows the previously modelled response, you might elicit the response by offering the child a choice where one response is that previously modelled. You hold up two items only one of which the child requires and ask, 'What do you want, the butter or the sugar?' Routines are followed carefully and the same words used. Once the routine is secure, you can unexpectedly change it so a response is necessary. You could give the child the butter but no bread, allowing plenty of time for his response.

Social stories

Social stories aim to help pupils understand the social environment and how to behave suitably in it, focusing on a desired outcome. As originally conceived (Gray, 1994), social stories are written by someone who knows the child well and concern a social situation the child finds difficult. The format includes descriptive, perspective and directive sentences. Descriptive sentences concern what happens, where it happens, who participates, what they do and why. Perspective sentences describe others' feelings and responses. Directive sentences provide guidance about what the pupil should try to do or say in the situation ('I should try to…'). Social stories should have more descriptive and perspective sentences than directive ones.

The pupil might write his own stories focused on matters and situations he finds difficult (Smith, 2003). He will discuss the developing story and the anticipation of the real life situations it describes. A comic strip format can be used with characters having speech/thought bubbles. Photographs and symbols can be employed. It is not always clear what social stories aim to achieve, whether they achieve it, which pupils benefit and whether any benefits persist.

Teaching language skills (and manual signing systems)

Autistic pupils may try to understand idioms through understanding the words not possible speaker intentions. You will need to explicitly teach aspects of conversational skills. These include using intonation, non-verbal communication (proximity to conversational partners), reducing echolalia and correcting the common reversal of pronouns ('You want a drink' when the message is 'I want a drink'). Approaches may use structured behavioural training but are likely to be protracted.

To increase spontaneous verbalisation for autistic children, you can use visual cue prompting such as coloured cards (Matson *et al.*, 1993), or time delay (Ingenmey and Van Houten, 1991; Matson *et al.*, 1993). When using time delay procedures to develop spontaneous requests the teacher might present the child with a target stimulus to be requested such as a toy. You immediately model the response (in this case a request for the item). When the child imitates the response without error you delay the prompting, and at each trial, lengthen the time delay. You reinforce a response whether spontaneous or imitated, by giving the child the item. As the stimulus/model interval increases, you expect the child to initiate the request independently before you give the prompt.

Many autistic children appear to have difficulties making manual signs and using them spontaneously (Attwood et al., 1988). However, the teacher may use signs to give an extra physical clue to what is being communicated.

Managing challenging behaviour

The context of autism can be influential in preventing and managing challenging behaviour where it occurs (Carr, 2006, p. 354). Autistic children perceive many situations, such as breaking into their routines, as frightening or threatening. They may find others' behaviour confusing and potentially distressing. Over-sensitivity to stimuli might lead an autistic child to react aggressively. Being unable to express wants and needs may exacerbate difficult behaviour. Behaviour may become a default system of communication in the absence of a more reliable system.

Important considerations are the environment in which the challenging behaviour occurs, what seems to precipitate it, the challenging behaviour itself and the response it elicits. Accordingly, the environment may be modified (as in structured teaching). You may refine what you request of the child. For example, obsessional behaviour may be prohibited generally, but, providing it is harmless and required tasks are finished, it may be allowed in recreation periods. Also you can convey certain behaviour is not tolerated as the Lovaas Programme 'excess' behaviour. The child can learn the consequences of actions by using communication aids and alternatives such as the Picture Exchange Communication System. Replacement behaviours may be taught which serve the same function as the problem behaviour.

Resources

Resources may be used to develop communication, for example the Picture Exchange Communication System. Visual timetables and other resources aimed at helping structure the environment may be used.

Therapy

Music therapy and art therapy used with autistic children have only limited supporting information for practice (Simpson, 2005). Musical interaction therapy (Prevezer, 2000) seeks to develop the child's ability to enjoy the company of others and his understanding of how to interact and communicate.

Wimpory and colleagues (1995) present a case study. They see normal communication as developing as the baby and familiar adult negotiate increasingly complex interactions in which the baby actively participates. As the baby responds to the adult and invites a response a dialogue develops. Accordingly, music interaction therapy involves the child's key worker or parent working with the autistic child, while a musician plays an instrument to support and encourage their interaction. The key worker might copy or join in with the child's actions as if the child intended these actions as communication so as to give the child experience of responses that would accompany intended communication.

Regarding medication, haloperidol can significantly decrease aggression and stereotypies, but has major side effects. Campbell *et al.* (1996) provide a review of its use with autistic children and adolescents.

Organisation

Physical organisation of the classroom

The physical organisation of the classroom is important in approaches such as structured teaching where physical structure adds meaning and context to the environment. For autistic children who are oversensitive to sensory stimulation in the environment, classroom areas that are quiet and have low visual stimulation may be used.

Working in pairs and groups

While autistic pupils find social situations difficult, much is learned in pairs or small groups in school. Drawing on behavioural principles, the autistic pupil can be taught individually by the teacher or teaching aide but in successively closer proximity to a small group of pupils. He can then work with one other child on a familiar task so efforts at adapting largely concern social aspects of the activity.

These activities can be made more appealing to autistic pupils by incorporating their special interest in the task or activity. The complexity of the task and level of social interaction required can be gradually increased. Next, the autistic pupil can be encouraged to work in a group of three pupils where again the task and social requirements can be gradually increased. Larger group work would follow. It is important the child also has some time alone or pursuing a preferred activity.

Learning Experiences – An Alternative Program for Preschoolers and Parents

Learning Experiences – An Alternative Program for Preschoolers and Parents (LEAP) (Strain and Hoyson, 2000) involves pre-schooling classes in which autistic children learn with typically developing children. parents are taught to use behavioural skills with their child at home and in the community. Typically developing peers are taught to help the social and language skills of children with autism; and data is collected each day on Individual Education Programme objectives to inform the next day's teaching plans.

The LEAP classroom might have about four children with autism and perhaps ten who do not and a special education teacher helps the children with autism throughout the day. The intention is that the autistic children have the opportunity to see models of appropriate social skills and more opportunities to interact with non-disabled peers.

Managing transitions

Because of an autistic child's resistance to change, major transitions are often particularly demanding. Starting school, moving to another school, moving home and moving from school to further or higher education require support (Jones, 2002, pp. 104–14).

Aids to successful transition include good local policies and procedures for transition, effective record keeping, good preparation for transfer and careful monitoring of the quality of procedures. The care taken with visual timetables and communication helps indicate to the child that a change is proposed from one activity to another, from one school area to another, from activity to leisure or from school to home.

Other aspects of provision

Family support and parent training

Initially, professionals should have explained autism to parents and helped them begin the process of understanding the disorder. Parents may welcome opportunities to ask questions, seek clarification, gain support or contact other parents with an autistic child. Family support including respite care and counselling, practical advice and training all help. Parent training is a part of many behavioural programmes. Parents can act as co-therapists, for example by using problem solving skills enabling them to better deal with current and future challenges.

The school can involve parents in setting and pursuing clear educational goals for children. Where goals are expressed in unambiguous behavioural terms, it is easier to identify progress and modify approaches where progress is disappointing. Families report wanting more information on *why* problem behaviours occur, how to help their child make choices, reducing family stress, sustaining energy levels and advocacy (Turnbull and Rueff, 1996).

THINKING POINTS

Readers may wish to consider with reference to a particular school:

- the extent to which application of the broad approach of structuring the environment is successful;
- the effectiveness of various approaches and the evidence on which they are based;
- the effectiveness of providing family support and training.

KEY TEXTS

Gabriels, R. and Hill, D. E. (2007) *Growing Up with Autism: Working with School Age Children and Adolescents* New York, Guilford Press.

This book provides guidance for supporting positive behaviour, social skills and communication and dealing with issues of mental and physical health and sexuality.

Wall, K. (2004) *Autism and Early Years Practice: A Guide for Early Years Professionals, Teachers and Parents* London, Paul Chapman.

This book contains a range of practical advice.

The Autism Society of America (www.autism-society.org) is a useful starting point for investigating other Internet sites.

Chapter 8

Conclusion

This chapter summarises the content of previous chapters. I draw together findings in relation to the curriculum and assessment, pedagogy, resources, therapy and school and classroom organisation. The chapter then outlines some foundational areas of special education.

Summary of previous chapters

In Chapter 1 'Introduction', I discussed the importance of the teacher and speech pathologist and others working closely together. Form and content in relation to communication was mentioned. I considered distinctions between language delay and language disorder. Implications of the terms 'impairment' and 'need' were discussed. The chapter examined a framework for communication disorders. I explained developmental verbal dyspraxia and dysarthria, and touched on aphasia, dysphasia, anomia, dysphonia and specific language impairment.

In Chapter 2 on 'Communication disorders: speech', I considered speech difficulties and their identification and assessment. I examined phonetic, prosodic and phonological aspects.

Chapter 3: 'Communication disorders: grammar' considered how grammar develops in children of different ages. I looked at causal factors. The chapter examined difficulties with syntax and morphology. I considered the assessment of grammar. I looked at provision to help grammar development.

In Chapter 4, 'Communication disorders: comprehension' I considered the nature of comprehension and how it develops. I then examined difficulties with comprehension. Assessment of comprehension was discussed. Provision to improve comprehension was examined.

Chapter 5, 'Communication disorders: semantics' looked at meaning in communication. I examined labelling, packaging and network building difficulties; difficulties with idiom; grammatical aspects of meaning; and meaning relations. After touching on the assessment of semantic difficulties, the chapter set out various aspects of provision.

In Chapter 6 'Communication disorders: pragmatics' I explained the nature of pragmatics and then considered pragmatic difficulties. The chapter looked at the assessment of such difficulties. I examined provision.

Chapter 7, 'Autism' described autism and explained the prevalence of autism and its apparent causes before looking at its identification and at provision.

Each chapter considered provision with regard to: the curriculum and assessment, pedagogy, resources, therapy and organisation.

Curriculum and assessment

The curriculum for pupils with speech disorders emphasises speaking and listening, as an activity in English lessons, as an aspect of other lessons, in structured sessions and through broader planning, cross curricular links and specific programmes. Phonological development may be assessed in small steps.

For grammar difficulties, the curriculum may emphasise grammar by planning to ensure sufficient time is spent on it, allocating extra curriculum time for selected pupils, using small group work within a whole class setting, and providing extra perhaps brief support and checking pupil's understanding. Grammar will be embedded in subjects across the curriculum and within certain subjects there may be a particular emphasis and support for grammar. Assessment may adopt small steps with regard to the development of grammar.

For difficulties with comprehension, the curriculum may increase the amount of time spent on developing the skills and understanding of comprehension, plan for comprehension in subjects across the curriculum; and emphasise supporting comprehension within most subjects. Good questioning and other methods used by the teacher can reveal a pupil's level of understanding. Assessment may adopt small steps with regard to the development of comprehension so that progress can be recognised and celebrated.

For difficulties with semantics, the curriculum may provide extra time, ensure that work supporting semantic development is embedded in cross-curricular planning with subjects across the curriculum and, within subjects, emphasise and support semantics. Assessment may adopt small steps with regard to the development of semantics. Literacy can introduce and give practice in common idioms and other aspects of meaning that all children may find especially difficult.

For difficulties with pragmatics, the curriculum may provide extra time for these aspects of communication, ensure work supporting pragmatic development is embedded in cross-curricular planning with subjects across the curriculum and, within subjects, provide emphasis and support for pragmatics. For a pupil having difficulty with conversational abstractions, planning of particularly implicated subjects includes activities to give practice in using potentially difficult expressions correctly. Assessment may adopt small steps.

For autistic pupils, the curriculum will be developmentally suitable and chronologically appropriate, and emphasise communication, social skills and play as well as academic skills training. Particular pedagogy is used to enable these aspects of curriculum content to be made meaningful and tolerable to the child. The curriculum incorporates the special interests of the autistic child to increase motivation, success and time spent on task. Curriculum based assessments and other assessments are interpreted with care.

Pedagogy

For pupils with speech disorders, pedagogy can include: raising phonological awareness, encouraging phonological change, error analysis and articulation exercises, cued articulation as a teaching support and alternative and augmentative communication.

Pedagogy for grammar difficulties may include: sentence recasting, elicited imitation, modelling and very clear class teacher communication. Pedagogy for comprehension difficulties includes: teaching for giving attention, teaching listening behaviour, reducing processing demands, supporting pragmatic understanding, allowing sufficient time to respond, and providing help with vocabulary.

Helping semantic labelling tasks involves: structured experience, explicit teaching, pretend play and using gesture or signs, graphic symbols, picture matching and printed labels. Regarding packaging tasks, interventions include: individual sessions to teach pupils to generalise or particularise, directly teaching from exemplars, modelling and reshaping the child's utterances. Networking is helped by: explicit teaching, encouraging semantic links, teaching words and explaining them in different subject contexts. To help with idiom, approaches include: examples and explanations, and explicit teaching. For difficulties with grammatical aspects of meaning, interventions are explanations and examples, specific teaching and support to develop understanding and play. Helping a child understand meaning relations involves practice and exemplars, structured experience and over-learning.

Pedagogy for pragmatic difficulties includes: providing basic skills and knowledge, and direct work with the speech and language pathologist in liaison with the teacher. Interventions to help with social and linguistic sense include being taught possible signals of the speaker's intentions and examples of implication and inference. Opportunities to use similar signals are provided in role-play and encouraged in day-to-day communication. For conversational skills, the child can be taught to recognise common opening gambits of an intention to start a new topic and respond accordingly. He can be taught to listen to possible signals that someone would like to change topic. He can also be taught the signals that the other person wants a turn. The teacher can teach the signs of conversation breakdown. Also the skills for repairing it can be taught and practised. The teacher or others may model suitable non-verbal communication. Pupils with semantic-pragmatic difficulties require help in the early years and at school. Support in the family is important.

Autistic children tend to respond to repeated brief structured sessions of teaching and learning drawing on behavioural and cognitive approaches. The focus is on sensitively building social interaction and communication skills. Approaches include: 'structured teaching', the Lovaas Programme, discrete trial teaching/training, pivotal response training, sensory integration, the Picture Exchange Communication System, the Children's Talk Project, joint action routines, social stories and explicit teaching of language skills. The teacher may use manual signing to help pupils understand. Where there is challenging behaviour a range of behavioural strategies may be used.

Resources

Resources used to help speech disorders, particularly where problems are severe, include: symbols, communication notebooks, communication grids, talking mats, communication aids for pupils with motor difficulties and dedicated communication devices. The development of grammar is supported by devices that can record and play back the pupil's language in different contexts so it can be analysed and used in subsequent remedial work.

Resources for comprehension difficulties include visual aids, encouraging the use of other sensory channels of communication to supplement auditory comprehension, helping pupils to build a vocabulary for sensory modes to provide further information about the pupil's experiences and the environment and relate it to language. For some pupils signing boards, communication boards and computer technology can assist comprehension. The development of semantics is supported by clear pictures to help with assessment and developing skills. A variety of objects are also used. In assessing pupils for pragmatic difficulties an audio or video recorder may be used. Also used are commercial tests, checklists and profiles and specific programmes, for example ones intended to help with social language. For autistic pupils, resources associated with developing communication may be used, for example the Picture Exchange Communication System. Visual timetables and other resources aimed at helping structure the environment may be used.

Therapy

For pupils with speech disorders, speech and language therapy is important. A psycholinguistic perspective may be used to inform assessments and interventions. Medical/surgical interventions are used for some speech disorders such as cleft palate.

Where a pupil has grammar difficulties, therapy may involve the speech and language pathologist working directly with pupils or working in a consultancy/monitoring role (or both). Direct work will ensure the pupil's vocabulary is sufficient and then encourage the development of correct grammatical utterances through modelling and allowing practice. This will be developed and reinforced as the speech pathologist works closely with the teacher, parents and others to encourage the correct use of grammar.

For comprehension difficulties the speech and language pathologist may work either directly with pupils or in a consultancy/monitoring role (or both). In individual sessions the speech pathologist may encourage the child to give proper attention to tasks and activities, and guide them to use listening skills and other skills that help comprehension. Through close liaison with the teacher and parents, these skills can be encouraged and applied in different contexts. Counselling may help some pupils vent frustrations and support pupils while the core difficulty of comprehension is tackled more directly by teachers.

For semantic difficulties, the speech and language pathologist may contribute through direct work with children or in a consultancy role or both. In one to one work, the speech pathologist will focus on semantic development. She may develop a programme in liaison with the teacher that the teacher or a classroom aide will deliver either one to one or in small group work.

For pragmatic difficulties, the speech and language pathologist's contribution may be through direct work with children. The pathologist may also work in a consultancy role, perhaps assessing the child, initiating joint-cally interventions and then liaising with the teacher to develop fuller scale programmes. Music therapy and art therapy are used with children with autism but both are associated with only limited supporting information. Musical interaction therapy may be used. Other aspects of provision for autistic pupils are family support and parental training.

Organisation

For pupils with speech disorders, the school may use environmental arrangement strategies, organise classrooms to ensure signing is seen and all pupils can be heard easily especially where the intelligibility of speech of some may be developing. For difficulties with grammar, opportunities for all pupils to develop speaking and listening are likely to benefit pupils with difficulties with grammar. Talking partners allow pupils to do this.

Where pupils have difficulties with comprehension, the teacher can signal the start of periods during which very careful listening is expected, designate an area for especially careful listening, use small groups where a classroom aide ensures careful attention and avoiding very long periods where attention is required. One-to-one work may be helpful for encouraging the development of semantics. Small group work also can enable the teacher or classroom aide to provide intensive support to help with meaning from time to time.

Classroom organisation to help pupils with the development of pragmatics includes opportunities to work individually from time to time with the teacher or a classroom aide, and opportunities for role play to teach and practise pragmatic skills.

For autistic pupils, the physical organisation of the classroom is important in approaches such as structured teaching where physical structure adds meaning and context to the environment. For autistic children who are oversensitive to sensory stimulation in the environment, classroom areas that are quiet and have low visual stimulation may be used. While social situations tend to be difficult for autistic pupils, much is learned in pairs or small groups in school. Learning Experiences – An Alternative Program for Preschoolers and Parents offers the opportunity for very young autistic children to learn with typically developing children. Transitions are managed with care.

A final word

The above summary of provision for different types of disability and disorder that have been examined in this book indicates the importance to schools of reviewing their curriculum, pedagogy, resources, organisation and therapy. In doing so schools will be able to ensure that provision helps encourage the best academic progress and the best personal and social development for their pupils.

Another essential aspect of special education that has been implicit throughout the book is that of professionals working closely with parents and other professionals. It is helpful to recognise the importance of professional contributions and the foundational disciplines that contribute to special education. Examples of these foundational disciplines are:

- legal/typological;
- terminological;
- social;
- medical;
- neuropsychological;
- psychotherapeutic;
- behavioural/observational;
- developmental;
- psycholinguistic;
- technological;
- pedagogical.

Legal/typological foundations of special education concern social, political and economic factors informing the context of special education legislation. It includes an understanding of current legislation and the main types of disabilities and disorders, drawing on classifications used in the systems in the country concerned. Terminological issues include the importance of terminology in special education; for example, 'needs', 'discrimination' and 'rights'. Social foundations include a social constructionist perspective. A social view of disability has been important in widening the understanding beyond individual factors. Medical influences involve the scope of the application of medical perspectives and the use of drugs in relation to children with disabilities and disorders.

Neuropsychological aspects draw on techniques used in neurological research and some uses of psychological and related tests in neuropsychology. Psychotherapeutic contributions involve systems approaches, psychodynamic perspectives and cognitive-behavioural standpoints. Behavioural/observational foundations consider behavioural approaches to learning with reference to learning theory and observational learning and modelling in social cognitive theory. Developmental features may draw on Piaget's theory of genetic epistemology, for example in relation to understandings of provision for children with cognitive impairment.

Psycholinguistic foundations involve frameworks incorporating input processing, lexical representations and output processing; and interventions. Technological aspects may explore how technology constitutes a foundation of special education through its enhancement of teaching and learning. Pedagogical aspects examine pedagogy in relation to special education, in particular the issue of distinctive pedagogy for different types of disabilities and disorders.

The book *Foundations of Special Education* (Farrell, 2009a) discusses these areas in detail.

Bibliography

Adams, C., Byers Brown, B. and Edwards, M. (1997) (2nd edition) *Developmental Disorders of Language* London, Whurr.

Aitchison, (1987) *Words in the Mind: An Introduction to the Mental Lexicon* Oxford, Basil Blackwell.

Akshoomoff, N. (Ed.) (2006) *Autism Spectrum Disorders* New York, Guilford Press.

Aldred, C., Green, J. and Adams, C. (2004) 'A new social communication intervention for children with autism: pilot randomised controlled treatment study suggesting effectiveness' *Journal of Child Psychology and Psychiatry* 45, 1420–30.

American Psychiatric Association (2000) *Diagnostic and Statistical Manual of Mental Disorders Fourth Edition, Text Revision (DSM-IV-TR)* Washington DC, APA.

Anderson-Wood, L. and Smith, B. R. (1997) *Working with Pragmatics: A Practical Guide to Promoting Communicative Competence* Bicester, Winslow Press.

Attwood *et al.* (1988) 'The understanding and use of interpersonal gestures by autistic and Down's syndrome children' *Journal of Autism and Developmental Disorders* 18, 241–57.

Bandura, A. (1977) *Social Learning Theory* Englewood Cliffs, NJ, Prentice-Hall.

——(1986) *Social Foundations of Thought and Action: A Social Cognitive Theory* Englewood Cliffs, NJ, Prentice-Hall.

Baron-Cohen, S. (2000) *Understanding Others' Minds* Oxford, Oxford University Press.

Bigge, J. L., Best, S. J. and Heller, K. W. (2001) (4th. edition) *Teaching Individuals with Physical, Health or Multiple Disabilities* Upper Saddle River, NJ, Merrill-Prentice Hall.

Bishop, D. V. M. (1997) *Uncommon Understanding: Development and Disorders of Understanding in Children* Hove, UK, Psychology Press.

——(2000) 'Pragmatic language impairment: a correlate of SLI, a distinct subgroup, or a part of the autistic continuum?' in Bishop, D. V. M. and Leonard, L. B. (2000) *Speech and Language Impairments in Children: Causes, Characteristics, Intervention and Outcome* Philadelphia, PA and Hove UK, Psychology Press.

Bishop, D. V. M. and Leonard, L. B. (Eds.) (2000) *Speech and Language Impairments in Children: Causes, Characteristics, Intervention and Outcome* Philadelphia, PA and Hove, UK, Psychology Press.

Bondy, A. S. and Frost, L. A. (1994) 'The Picture Communication System' *Focus on Autistic Behaviour* 9, 3, 1–9.

Cain, K. and Oakhill, J. (Eds.) (2007) *Children's Comprehension Problems in Oral and Written Language: A Cognitive Perspective* New York, Guilford Press.

Campbell, M., Schopler, E., Cueva, J. E. and Hallin, A. (1996) 'Treatment of autistic disorder' *Journal of the American Academy for Child and Adolescent Psychiatry* 35, 134–43.

Carr, A. (2006) (2nd edition) *The Handbook of Child and Adolescent Clinical Psychology: A Contextual Approach* London, Routledge.

Case-Smith, J. and Bryant, T. (1999) 'The effects of occupational therapy with sensory integration emphasis on preschool age children wit autism' *American Journal of Occupational Therapy* 53, 489–97.

Cockerill, H. and Carrollfew, L. (2007) *Communicating without Speech: Practical Augmentative and Alternative Communication for Children* New York, Blackwell Publishers.

Committee on Educational Interventions for Children with Autism (2001) *Educating Children with Autism* Washington, DC, National Academy Press.

Dean, E., Howell, J. and Waters, D. (1990) *Metaphon Resource Pack* Windsor, NFER-Nelson.

Department of Education and Skills (2005) (2nd edition) *Data Collection by Special Educational Need* London, DfES.

Dockrell, J., Messer, D., George, R. and Wilson, G. (1998) 'Children with word finding difficulties – prevalence, presentation and naming problems' *International Journal of Language and Communication Disorders* 33, 4, 445–54.

Ellis Weismer, S. and Schrader, T. (1993) 'Discourse characteristics and verbal reasoning: wait time effects on the performance of children with language learning disabilities' *Exceptionality Education Canada* 3, 71–92.

Farrell, M. (2009a) *Foundations of Special Education* London, Wiley.

——(2009b) *The Special Education Handbook* London, David Fulton Publishers.

Fey, M. E. and Proctor-Williams, K. (2000) 'Recasting, elicited imitation and modelling in grammar intervention for children with specific language impairment' in Bishop, D. V. M. and Leonard, L. (Eds.) *Intervention and Outcome* New York, Psychology Press.

Firth, C. and Venkatesh, K. (2001) *Semantic-Pragmatic Language Disorder* Brackley, UK, Speechmark.

Flynn, L. and Lancaster, G. (1997) *Children's Phonology Sourcebook* Brackley, UK, Speechmark Publishing.

Fonteneau, E. and van der Lely H. K. J. (2008) 'Electrical brain responses in language-impaired children reveal grammar-specific deficits' *PLoS ONE* 3, 3, e1832. doi:10.1371/journal.pone.0001832.

Foster, S. H. (1990) *The Communicative Competence of Young Children: A Modular Approach* New York, Longman.

Gabriels, R. and Hill, D. E. (2007) *Growing Up with Autism: Working with School Age Children and Adolescents* New York, Guilford Press.

Gagnon, L., Mottron, L. and Jonette, Y. (1997) 'Questionning the validity of the Semantic-Pragmatic Syndrome diagnosis' *Autism* 1, 37–55.

Gillberg, C. and Coleman, M. (2000) (2nd edition) *The Biology of the Autistic Syndromes* London, McKeith Press.

Gillberg, C., Steffenburg, S. and Schaumann, H. (1991) 'Is autism more common now than ten years ago?' *British Journal of Psychiatry* 30, 489–94.

Gray, C. (1994) *The Social Stories Book* Arlington TX, Future Horizons.

Howell, J. and Dean, E. (1994) (2nd edition) *Treating Phonological Disorders in Children – Metaphon – Theory to Practice* London, Whurr Publishers.

Humphries, T. L. (2003) 'Effectiveness of pivotal response training as a behavioural intervention for young children with autism spectrum disorders' *Bridges Practice Based Research Synthesis* 2, 4, 1–10.

Hunt, J. and Slater, A. (2003) *Working with Children's Voice Disorders* Brackley, UK, Speechmark.

Ingenmey, R. and Van Houten, R. (1991) Using time delay to promote spontaneous speech in an autistic child' *Journal of Applied Behaviour Analysis* 24, 591–96.

Jones, G. (2002) *Educational Provision for Children with Autism and Asperger's Syndrome: Meeting Their Needs* London, David Fulton Publishers.

Kaiser, A. P. (2000) 'Teaching functional communication skills' in Snell, M. E. and Brown, F. (Eds.) (5th edition) *Instruction of Students with Severe Disabilities* Upper Saddle River, NJ, Merrill/Prentice Hall, pp. 453–92.

Kanner, L. (1943) 'Autistic disturbances of affective contact' *Nervous Child* 2, 217–50.

Kauffman, J. M. and Hallahan, D. P. (2005) *Special Education: What It Is and Why We Need It* Boston, MA, Pearson/Allyn and Bacon.

Kersner, M. and Wright, J. (Eds.) (2001) *Speech and Language Therapy: The Decision Making Process when Working with Children* London, David Fulton Publishers.

Kirby, A. and Drew, S. (2003) *Guide to Dyspraxia and Developmental Co-ordination Disorders* London, David Fulton Publishers.

Koegel, L. K. and Koegel, R. L. (1995) 'Motivating communication in children with autism' in Schopler, E. and Mezibov, G. (Eds.) *Learning and Cognition in Autism: Current Issues in Autism* New York, Plenum Press, pp. 73–87.

Laine, M. and Martin, N. (2006) *Anomia: Theoretical and Clinical Aspects* New York, Routledge.

Lancaster, G. and Pope, L. (1997) *Working with Children's Phonology* Brackley, UK, Speechmark.

Law, J., Lindsay, G., Peacey, N., Gascoigne, M., Soloff, N., Radford, J., Band, S. with Fitzgerald, L. (2000) *Provision for Children with Speech and Language Needs in England and Wales: Facilitating Communication Between Education and Health Services* London, Department for Education and Employment Research, report RR239.

Lawson, W. (1998) *Life Behind the Glass: A Personal Account of Autistic Spectrum Disorder* Lismore, Aus., Southern Cross University Press.

Leonard, L. (1998) *Children with Specific Language Impairment* Cambridge, MA: MIT Press.

Liberman, I. Y., Shankweiler, D. and Liberman, A. M. (1989) 'The alphabetic principle in learning to read' in Shankweiler, D. and Liberman, I. Y. (Eds.) *Phonology and Reading Disability: Solving the Reading Puzzle* Ann Arbour, MI, University of Michigan Press.

Locke, A., Ginsborg, J. and Peers, I. (2002) 'Development and disadvantage: implications for the early years and beyond' *International Journal of Language and Communication* Disorders 37, 1, 3–15.

Lord, C. and Schopler, E. (1987) 'Neurobiological implications of sex differences in autism' in Schopler, E. and Mezibov, G. (Eds.) *Neurobiological Issues in Autism* New York, Plenum.

Lord, C. *et al.* (2000) 'The Autism Diagnostic Observation Schedule – Generic: a standard measure of social and communication deficits associated with the spectrum of autism' *Journal of Autism and Developmental Disorders* 30, 3, 205.

Lovaas, O. I. (1987) 'Behavioural treatment and normal intellectual and educational functioning in autistic children' *Journal of Consulting and Clinical Psychology* 55, 3–9.

MacKay, G. and Anderson, C. (Eds.) (2000) *Teaching Children with Pragmatic Difficulties of Communication: Classroom Approaches* London, David Fulton Publishers.

Martin, D. (2000) *Teaching Children with Speech and Language Difficulties* London, David Fulton Publishers.

Martin, D. and Miller, C. (2003) *Speech and Language Difficulties in the Classroom* London, David Fulton Publishers.

Martin, D. and Reilly, O. (1995) 'Global language delay: analysis of a severe central auditory processing deficit' in Perkins, M. and Howard, S. (Eds.) *Case Studies in Clinical Linguistics* London, Whurr.

Matson, J. L., Sevin, J. A., Box, M. L. and Francis, K. L. (1993) 'An evaluation of two methods for increasing self-initiated verbalisations in autistic children' *Journal of Applied Behaviour Analysis* 26, 389–96.

Medical Research Council (2001) *Review of Autism Research: Epidemiology and Causes* London, Medical Research Council (www.mrc.ac.uk).

Mesibov, G. B. (1988) 'Diagnosis and assessment of autistic adolescents and adults' in Schopler, E. and Mesibov, G. B. (Eds.) *Diagnosis and Assessment in Autism* New York: Plenum Press, pp. 227–38.

Mesibov, G. B. and Howley, M. (2003) *Accessing the Curriculum for Pupils with Autistic Spectrum Disorders: Using the TEACCH Programme to Help Inclusion* London, David Fulton Publishers.

Milloy, N. and MorganBarry, R. (1990) 'Developmental neurological disorders' in Grunwell, P. (Ed.) *Developmental Speech Disorders* London, Whurr Publishers.

Mundy, P. and Neale, A. (2001) 'Neural plasticity, joint attention and a transactional social-orienting of autism' in Glidden, L. (Ed.) *International Review of Research in Mental Retardation. Autism* vol. 23, San Diego, CA, Academic Press, pp. 139–68.

Ozonoff, S. (1997) 'Components of executive function in autism and other disorders' in Russell, J. *Autism as an Executive Disorder* Oxford, Oxford University Press.

Pascoe, M., Stackhouse, J. and Wells, B. (2006) *Persisting Speech Difficulties in Children Book 3: Children's Speech and Literacy Difficulties* London, Wiley.

Paul, R. (2007) *Language Disorders from a Developmental Perspective: Essays in Honor of Robin S. Chapman* New York, Taylor & Francis.

Prevezer, W. (2000) 'Musical interaction and children with autism' in Powell, S. (Ed.) *Helping Children with Autism to Learn* London, David Fulton Publishers.

Prizant, B. M. and Wetherby, A. M. (1993) 'Communication in pre-school autistic children' in Schopler, E. *et al.* (Eds.) *Preschool Issues in Autism* New York, Plenum.

Prizant, B., Wetherby, A. and Rydell, P. (2000) 'Communication intervention issues for children with autism spectrum disorders' in Wetherby, A. M. and Prizant, B. M. (Eds.) *Autism Spectrum Disorders: A Transactional Development Perspective* vol. 9, Baltimore, MD, Brookes.

Reynolds, C. R. and Fletcher-Janzen, E. (Eds.) (2004) (2nd edition) *Concise Encyclopaedia of Special Education: A Reference for the Education of Handicapped and Other Exceptional Children and Adults* Hoboken, NY, John Wiley and Sons.

Rice, M. L. (2000) 'Grammatical symptoms of specific language impairments' in Bishop, D. V. M. and Leonard, L. B. *Speech and Language Impairments in Chldren: Causes, Characteristics, Intervention and Outcome* Philadelphia, PA and Hove, UK, Psychology Press.

Rinaldi, W. (2001) *Social Use of Language Programme* Windsor, NFER-Nelson.

Ripley, K. and Barrett, J. (2008) *Supporting Speech, Language and Communication Needs* Los Angeles and London, Sage.

Rutter, M. (1996) 'Autism research: prospects and priorities' *Journal of Autism and Development Disorders* 26, 2, 257–75.

Schneiderman, C. R. and Potter, R. E. (2002) *Speech-Language Pathology: A Simplified Guide to Structures, Functions and Clinical Implications* San Diego CA, Academic Press.

Schopler, E. (1997) 'Implementation of TEACCH philosophy' in Cohen, D. and Volkmar, F. (Eds.) (2nd edition) *Handbook of Autism and Pervasive Developmental Disorders* New York, Wiley, pp. 767–95.

Schwartz, R. G. (2007) *The Handbook of Child Language Disorders* New York, Routledge.

Sewell, K. (2000) *Breakthroughs: How to Reach Students with Autism* Verona, WI, Attainment Company.

Simpson, R. L. (2005) 'Evidence based practices and students with ASD' *Focus on Autism and Other Developmental Disabilities* 20, 3, 140–49.

Smith, C. (2003) *Writing and Developing Social Stories: Practical Interventions in Autism* Oxford, Harcourt Assessment.

Stacey, K. (1994) 'Contextual assessment of young children: moving from the strange to the familiar and from theory to praxis' *Child Language Teaching and Therapy* 10, 2, 179–98.

Stackhouse, J. and Wells, B. (1997) *Children's Speech and Literacy Difficulties Book 1: A Psycholinguistic Framework* London, Whurr Publishing.

——(2001) *Children's Speech and Literacy Difficulties Book 2: Identification and Intervention* London, Whurr Publishing.

Strain, P. and Hoyson, M. (2000) 'The need for longitudinal, intensive social skill intervention: LEAP follow-up outcomes for children with autism' *Topics in Early Childhood Special Education* 20, 2, 116–22.

Stewart, T. and Turnbull, J. (2007) *Working with Dysfluent Children* Brackley, UK, Speechmark.

Tallal, P. (2000) 'Experimental studies of language learning impairments: from research to remediation' in Bishop, D. V. M. and Leonard, L. B. (2000) *Speech and Language Impairments in Children: Causes, Characteristics, Intervention and Outcome* Philadelphia, PA and Hove, UK, Psychology Press.

Tesak, J. and Code, C. (2007) *Milestones in the History of Aphasia: Theories and Protagonists* Hove, UK and New York, NY.

Thompson, G. (2003) *Supporting Children with Communication Disorders: A Handbook for Teachers and Teaching Assistants* London, David Fulton Publishers.

Townsend, D. (1997) *An Introduction to Aesthetics* Malden, MA and Oxford, Blackwell.

Turnbull A. and Rueff, M. (1996) 'Family perspectives on problem behaviour' *Mental Retardation*, 34, 5, 280–93.

Vanderheiden, G. C. and Lloyd, L. L. (1986) 'Communication systems and their components' in Blackstone, S. W. and Bruskin, D. M. (Eds.) *Augmentative Communication: An Introduction* Rockville, MD, American Speech-Language-Hearing Association, pp. 29–162.

van der Lely, H. (1994) 'Canonical linking rules: forward versus reverse thinking in normally developing and language impaired children' *Cognition* 51, 29–72.

Volkmar, F. R. and Nelson, D. (1990) 'Seizure disorders in autism' *Journal of the American Academy for Child and Adolescent Psychiatry* 29, 127–29.

Wall, K. (2004) *Autism and Early Years Practice: A Guide for Early Years Professionals, Teachers and Parents* London, Paul Chapman.

Walley, A. C. (1993) 'The role of vocabulary development in children's spoken word recognition and segmentation ability' *Developmental Review* 13, 286–350.

Watson, I. (1991) 'Phonological processing in two languages' in Bailystok, E. (Ed.) *Language Processing in Bilingual Children* Cambridge, Cambridge University Press.

Wells, G. (1985) *Language Development in the Preschool Years* Cambridge, Cambridge University Press.

Wimpory, D. *et al.* (1995) 'Musical interaction therapy for children with autism: an illustrative case study with a two year follow up' Brief report *Journal of Autism and Developmental Disorders* 25, 541–42.

Wing, L. and Gould, J. (1979) 'Severe impairments of social interaction and assorted abnormalities in children: Epidemiology and classification' *Journal of Autism and Childhood Schizophrenia* 9, 11–29.

Wing, L., Leekham, S., Libby, S., Gould, J. and Larcombe, M. (2002) 'The diagnostic interview for social and communication disorders: background, inter-rater reliability and clinical use' *Journal of Child Psychology and Psychiatry* 43, 307–25.

Wray, A. (2001) 'Formulaic sequences in second language teaching: principle and practice' *Applied Linguistics* 21, 4, 463–89.

Index

abstract concepts 47, 48, 52
address, forms of 59, 63
aided communication 17–19
alternative and augmentative
  communication 17
American Psychiatric Association 4–5,
  6, 67
American Speech-Language-Hearing
  Association 57
anomia 7
antonyms 47, 52
aphasia 7
applied behaviour analysis
  72–73
apraxia of speech *see* developmental
  verbal dyspraxia
attention difficulties 35, 36
auditory aids 16
auditory discrimination 19
auditory memory 26
auditory sequential memory 25
autism: diagnosis and causal factors
  67–69; family support and training
  78–79; identification and assessment
  69–70; resources 76, 84; teaching
  strategies 70–76, 83; therapy and
  medication 77; transition, managing
  78; working in groups 77–78
Autism Genome Project 68
autistic spectrum disorder 2

behavioural and emotional problems
  11–12, 30, 35, 76
bilingual children 12, 37, 61
brain damage 6, 34

Carrollfew, L *see* Cockerill, H
causal factors: autism 68–69;
  grammar 24; pragmatic difficulties
  60–61
challenging behaviour 76
Children's Phonology Sourcebook 16
Children's Talk Project 74
classroom organisation 20, 42, 54, 65,
  77–78, 85
cleft lip/palate 13
Cockerill, H 21
cognitive process 34, 45–46
communication facilitation
  techniques 62
communication grid 18
communication notebook 18
comprehension: classroom organisation
  42; definition and process of 33–34;
  development and difficulties 34–36;
  identification and assessment 36–37;
  resources 41–42, 83; teaching
  strategies 37–42, 82; therapy 42
computer aids 18–19, 42, 83
conjunctions 58
connectors 31
constituents 22, 23–24
contextual clues 47, 52
conversational skills 59, 60, 64–65,
  75–76
curriculum and assessment: autism
  69–70, 82; comprehension skills 36,
  37, 81; grammar development 28,
  81; phonological skills 15, 81;
  pragmatic difficulties 61, 82;
  semantic difficulties 50, 81

Printed in the USA/Agawam, MA
March 15, 2013

573667.110